Shopped

A True Story of Secret Shopping and Self-Discovery

EMILY STOTT

s epte
m
b
er

1 3 5 7 9 10 8 6 4 2

First published in 2016 by September Publishing

Text and illustrations copyright © Emily Stott 2016

Printed in Poland on paper from responsibly managed,
sustainable sources by Hussar Books

ISBN 978-1-910463-30-7

September Publishing
www.septemberpublishing.org

CONTENTS

Author's Note

This book is the true story of my experiences in the world of retail. Some names and other details have been changed in order to protect privacy and confidentiality.

The Vertiginous High Heels

I knew it was a mistake to wear these shoes. Vertiginous, sleek and an absolute bargain to boot, they look great, and they're perfect for the role I'm about to play, but they're about as impractical as you can get, as I have discovered after an eight-minute sprint to the station. I should have stuffed some pumps into my bag but the rolled-up copy of *Elle* poking out of one end of my equally unsuitable bag took priority. To add insult to injury I have to stand for the duration of the tube journey and my feet are starting to throb. It's 10 a.m. I balance, flamingo-style, on one spike heel, bending the other foot up to meet my hand so I can massage my crushed toes.

I see my reflection through a gap in the bowed commuter heads. I look distinctly dishevelled – this was not part of the plan, my character simply doesn't have the time for untidiness in her life. In a futile attempt to look groomed I tuck the stray sections of hair springing from my temples back behind my ears. I should have worn a hat. My hair never does what it's supposed to do and today I needed it to look neat. Damn, a hat would have been just right for my character too. Perhaps I should buy one on my way from the station? But then I'll be ten quid down before I've even got to where I'm going. This is to be a frugal month, which means swapping the Pret sandwiches for my crap home-made ones and staying away from sample sales. Otherwise, there will be no summer holiday this year.

I sigh, prompting a tut from a fellow passenger who doesn't even look up from her *Metro*. Her black coat completely drains her face of colour, a pale blue would have been so much better, however it doesn't seem as if this lady is looking forward to a pale-blue kind of day. Funny how the female half of the population relies so heavily on black, I don't think I've ever heard a bloke opting for a black garment 'because it's slimming'. I grin as I'm reminded of the on-going debate I have with a friend about his awful orange jumper. Oh, I may not look like I know stuff, with my messy hair and silly shoes, but I do.

I pull my bag closer to my side as I step carefully down the station steps, sensibly shod commuters rushing past me on either side. Today I am going to be one of them: a successful, self-assured businesswoman on the lookout for expensive new shoes. I set off down Sloane Street, the confident stride in my step belying my concern over a bad hair day. Chauffeur-driven cars with blacked-out windows sit on single yellow lines, awaiting their passengers who will eventually emerge laden down with purchases. What must that be like, I wonder? I am not one of those shoppers, not today or any day.

A beautiful evening dress catches my eye and, as I stand back and admire it sparkling in its spotlight, and looking otherworldly on this blustery autumn day, I can't help but imagine myself in it, posing on a red carpet, the possibility of an award mere minutes away. I turn to look at my reflection side on, chin perched on one shoulder, to check there are no ladders in my tights. Do I look the part? I mustn't be found out: calling the client to say my cover has been blown is not an option. I have worked hard to earn a reputation for being reliable and thorough, and I'm not about to throw it away on account of my costume. I lean further towards the polished glass to check my teeth, so immersed in my own thoughts that at first I fail to notice the member of staff on the other side of the twinkling mannequin, looking curiously at me as I study myself, teeth bared.

Embarrassed, I move quickly on. As I approach my destination I reapply my lipstick, run my fingers through my hair one last time, smile my rehearsed high-flying smile to myself and graciously purr 'Good morning' to the looming security guard as he pulls open the door for me.

The smell of freshly polished mirrors and the softest buttery leather fills the air. 'Good morning, how are you today?' asks the pretty woman, who smiles warmly as she approaches me, not a hair out of place, regulation flat pumps on her feet. 'Can I help you?'

I take a deep breath. 'I certainly hope so . . .'

CHAPTER ONE

The Navy-Blue Anorak with Red Trim

1972 was quite a year. Edward Heath was prime minister, *The French Connection* won the Academy Award for best film, David Bowie introduced Ziggy Stardust to the world and Stan Smith won the men's singles championship at Wimbledon. That same month, London saw its first Gay Pride march and *Are You Being Served?* – based on the Simpson's Department Store in Piccadilly – was the programme everyone watched on the box. It was also the year that the French Connection clothes chain and *Cosmopolitan* magazine were launched.

I too arrived in 1972, in March and nine days late, a first baby for my parents and a first granddaughter following five grandsons, for my maternal grandparents. When my twenty-four-year-old mum woke with tummy pains the day before I was born, she put it down to having eaten something dodgy and set off to do some shopping. It was my mum's school friend Heather, a nurse like my mum, who suggested that perhaps it might be an idea to call the hospital. Luckily Heather had been listening that day at medical school otherwise I might have been born on a shop floor somewhere.

My parents Richard and Penny met in 1965 and married five years later. They had both moved to London to embark on their careers. My dad's job as an investigative reporter on the *Daily Mirror* and my mum's nursing training at London's Middlesex Hospital meant they worked shifts and they shared a small flat at 166 Finchley Road in north London with Val, one of Mum's nursing friends.

My aunt Judith – Jude – an actress, had married her second husband, the comedian Dave Allen, in 1964 after a whirlwind romance in Australia where both were working. David had made a name for himself on television there, but when Jude returned to England, where she had a young son and a successful acting career, he followed her back. My dad was introduced to David shortly before he met my mum. The two of them got on famously; David's father had worked at the *Irish Times* but more importantly my dad and David shared a wicked sense of humour. Dad ended up asking David to be his best man. To the thrill of my twenty-two-year-old mum, this meant that on the first day of their Paris honeymoon, a photograph of their rain-soaked wedding (my mum beaming broadly in between these two small, dark and handsome men) appeared in the *Sunday Express*.

My mum claims that she, Val and Penny, another nursing friend, were the first to strut down the King's Road in Chelsea in miniskirts. Whether or not this is true, there is certainly evidence that in 1970 these three wore skirts barely covering their bottoms to a wedding. It wouldn't be considered either suitable or stylish now (was I the only one quietly indignant when Kate Moss wore hot pants to a friend's wedding?), but the more relaxed attitudes of the 1960s had made their mark and paved the way for yet more sartorial experimentation. A nurse's salary didn't allow for huge shopping expeditions but these girls were resourceful, borrowing each other's clothes, giving each other face masks and doing each other's hair, and occasionally even making their own clothes. My mum had a curvy body shape, and as the bikinis on the high street simply didn't cater to her measurements – at least not in a way she liked – she set about making her own, under-wiring and all. It was one way of avoiding the embarrassment of trying on swimwear, and the only way to ensure a perfect fit for the bottom and the top. A lady of many talents, my mum.

My dad travelled a lot (only narrowly escaping missing my sister's premature birth) with his job for the *Mirror*, often returning with pieces he had picked up along the way – a blue-and-white seersucker suit here, an orange-and-purple silk scarf there. On one occasion, when he went to New York accompanied by my mum, they bought me and my sister matching blue nightdresses from Bloomingdale's. You really couldn't tell whose excitement at their swag was bigger, ours or theirs. Dad loved New York and assured me I would do too. 'It's the one place in the world where it is exactly as you imagine it to be,' he told me, 'just as it is in the films.'

So often labelled 'the decade that style forgot', the 1970s that I arrived into was anything but. Photographs and films of this time show it to be alive with colour and expression, a happy time, assured enough to finally lay the sixties to rest.

This was a confident time in fashion history when actresses like Diane Keaton and Jane Fonda were breaking the very girly mould with their eclectic fashion choices. Woody Allen wrote *Annie Hall* specifically for Diane Keaton, who adopted her own very individual personal style for the title role. The bowler hat, waistcoat and tie, wide trousers and lace-up shoes ensemble assured the actress style-icon status, not an obvious label for a low-key comedy actress with a slightly awkward walk. At the opposite end of the scale, Jane Fonda had already made a name for herself in the sixties with the release of the cult film *Barbarella*. Her skintight catsuit became the stuff of fashion legend and propelled her to stardom. Attention was focused not only on her acting talents but also on her wardrobe choices, and by the mid-seventies Fonda had won her first Oscar for the film *Klute* as well as a following of women copying her style of thigh high boots, polonecks and miniskirts.

It was an exciting time of change in British fashion with a shift away from the very relaxed vibe of the sixties. Clothes were exaggerated – jeans were more flared than ever, skirts and collars were longer, ties were wider. Simultaneously, late-nineteenth-century detailing like ruffles, flounces, lace and puffed sleeves started to appear and it was this aesthetic that put Laura Ashley, who had started out as a soft furnishings designer, firmly on the map. For almost a decade, long white cotton dresses and blouses evocative of nightwear sold like hot cakes. The Fulham branch of Laura Ashley sold 4,000 dresses in one week alone. The floor-length polka-dot dress and floppy hat my mum wore for my sister's christening was pure elegance, utterly impractical for a mother of a newborn running around after a toddler, but fabulous for that one day.

For those of us who grew up in the seventies, life was a series of hot hazy summers and snowy Christmases negotiated in striped skinny-ribbed polonecks and corduroy trousers. You buckled your roller skates over your T-bar shoes and huge strawberry Mivvi ice lollies cost no more than 25p. We were outside on our bikes as much as we could, the only reason to be inside being to sleep, bathe or do homework – but who wanted to do any of those things? I was either dressed up folk-style as Laura Ingalls Wilder from *Little House on the Prairie* (the Laura Ingalls Wilder portrayed in the television series was someone lots of little girls were slightly obsessed with then) or in nothing but a sun hat and wellies, the easiest and most pull-on-able garments a small child can find. At home we had one television (it was white; Mum was rather taken aback when Dad came home with it) and were the last family I knew to get a video recorder. I lived for Friday mornings when my *Bunty* comic arrived along with the rest of the day's newspapers – and there were at least seven of them. Our paperboy lugged every single publication every single day to our house. He then squeezed each newspaper through the letterbox, which then landed with a loud thud onto the floor below. Eventually, my dad asked the newsagent if the paperboy could perhaps, to save time, leave the pile on the doormat outside.

Newsprint was highly transferable in those days and on the weekends when my dad took the papers back to bed with him and we all bundled in, the bed sheets would end up smeared with black. No wonder my mum invested in some teal-coloured bed linen – funky but practical. Dad's black fingerprints would also end up on all the light switches and door knobs and my poor mum would follow his inky trail with a J-cloth. If you spent any time at all in our house it wasn't unusual to leave with a smudge of newspaper print on your nose. You might also be sent off with a copy of the *Daily Mirror* under your arm, Dad never missed an opportunity to spread his written word.

In 1974, just before my sister was born, my parents decided to move our little family of three from the rented flat above the junk shop in north London to leafy Kingston-upon-Thames, just to the south.

My parents decided to make the move from north to south London mainly because David and Jude had a house in Ham where they lived with their four children. Eventually, however, with Jude no longer acting, they made the move out of London and we would visit them at their beautiful home in Henley. My aunt Jude was not one to do anything by halves and we would arrive in Henley to find their house stuffed full of people of all ages. Many of them would invariably be theatre friends. I didn't give a second thought to the presence of Maggie Smith, Peter Hall and John Gielgud, they were simply older people with loud projecting voices. If I had known the pedigree I was surrounded by perhaps I would have thought twice about forcing them all to sit and watch my self-penned playlets of which I was more often than not the star. The theatrical tales, both overheard and told to me, along with the glamour of those weekends, helped to infect me with the acting bug even though my aunt had taken a step back from acting right at the peak of her career.

To a small child, their house was like a fairy-tale castle and my imagination ran riot whenever we visited. I would happily explore the grounds for hours dressed as a cowgirl or occasionally Queen Elizabeth I. Aunt Jude appeared to have stolen costumes from every job she ever had. The enormous attic, which was home to two rocking horses among other things, had a vast walk-in wardrobe containing costumes from Cinderella to Captain Hook. It would be exciting for any little girl but for me it was heaven on earth.

It wasn't every Saturday my dad and I were left to our own devices but this particular Saturday was unusual. The evening before, just before opening time on 14 March 1975 and three weeks ahead of schedule, my new baby sister came into the world. I wasn't fazed by the sudden disappearance of my mum because having my dad left in charge meant fish and chips for supper and a far later bedtime. Then on Saturday morning we went shopping, just him and me. I was three years and six days old and I needed a new anorak. My dad took my hand and we walked into Kingston town centre to check out the anoraks in Bentalls. Later that day, one new navy-blue anorak with red floral trim purchased, we found the time to go to the hospital to meet Hannah, my new sibling.

The Bentalls department store of my childhood was not as it is today, conjoined to a big shopping mall and bordering a pedestrianised town centre. In 1975 there were no balloon sellers or musicians in Kingston town centre, no one selling the *Big Issue* and no McDonald's or Starbucks. Instead, a coffee break was likely to be taken in either the Bentalls or BHS cafes – soulless places filled with old ladies in hats sipping tea, nibbling Bourbon biscuits and *moaning* about Sainsbury's running out of syrup of figs. C&A was still around then. Traffic drove right down the high street making it a bit of a squeeze on the pavements on a Saturday (the one really big shopping day), and there were perhaps two car parks compared to the nine or ten there are now.

My mum was a nurse, slim, young and pretty, and naturally I wanted to be just like her. I couldn't wait until I was tall enough to be able to run up the stairs two at a time as she always did, to deftly reverse into a parking space with a strong quick twist of the steering wheel. Mum's biceps were well honed, probably due to lifting heavy patients in and out of bed, although it seemed to me it was more likely a direct result of the daily steering wheel workout. When Mum got ready for an evening out with my dad, I would lie on their bed watching her apply make-up and deciding what to wear, fascinated by those things that I would only have access to 'when you're grown up': high-heeled shoes (not so high in the seventies), colourful lipsticks and eye shadows, and long silky scarves. Mum didn't spend hours getting ready – she didn't have the time – but she would leave the house looking effortlessly lovely. If I was ever sad to see her go, I don't remember it, but Mum being out of the house meant one thing: an uninterrupted opportunity to go through her wardrobe.

I did not realise it then but this was the start of my fascination with how we present ourselves to the world. Clothes are powerful, and while the psychology of fashion, or rather style, is inextricably linked to factors out of our control, such as the weather, where we are going and what we will be doing there, the clothes we choose speak volumes about how we perceive ourselves. Then there are our complicated thoughts and feelings which affect the way we move, act and communicate. By the time mood, body confidence, happiness and health have been added to the mix, it's no wonder that sometimes it can take so long to get dressed. And that's without trends and personal taste coming into it.

I loved that navy-blue anorak with the red trim and each time it was handed down to the next three-year-old in line, I thought of that shopping trip with my dad, me excitedly skipping back along the river and him making me laugh until I hiccoughed at his duck impressions, the shiny green Bentalls bag swinging as we went.

Kingston's town centre was a cut above the sort of thing you found in most towns and people travelled a significant distance to shop there. We were fortunate in the choice we had in Kingston. Even then, friends who lived outside Greater London could only dream of being able to shop at somewhere like Chelsea Girl. C&A, BHS and M&S were the standard destinations for kidswear, with the dreaded school shoes determinedly Clark's or Start-Rite. The little railway station, strangely old-fashioned for such a thriving town centre, groaned under the weight of the enthusiastic Saturday shoppers.

There were a wide variety of shoe shops such as Lilley and Skinner, Ravel, Dolcis, and Freeman, Hardy and Willis in addition to Bentalls department store, I grew up with a pretty good idea of which store sold what (swimwear at BHS, fabric at Bentalls, knickers from M&S, ski-wear at C&A) and went on regular shopping trips with my mum. My mum shopped in Hennes and so that was where I started too. Clothes shops for children were few and far between and the Hennes in Kingston stocked reasonably priced childrenswear.

According to my mum, from a very young age I made a beeline for anything bright and sparkly, sometimes adding items to the pram containing my sleeping sister, without Mum noticing. I wasn't immune to throwing a tantrum over a pair of wedge-heeled gold mules picked out of the bargain bin at Freeman, Hardy and Willis. Mum didn't stand any nonsense. 'When you're grown up you can buy as many silly shoes as you like but while I'm in charge and your feet are still growing, you will wear sensible shoes.' The same went for brushing my teeth and going to bed at a reasonable hour. She knew best, and I was going to have to wait a very long time indeed before I would be allowed to ruin my feet, let my teeth rot and develop dark shadows under my eyes. How totally unreasonable!

Bentalls department store was a fairly sombre affair when I was a child. It seemed fusty and boring to me, and I couldn't understand why grown-ups wanted to spend what seemed like hours browsing through their racks of clothes. After I was caught shoplifting by my granny (two plastic rings that were way too big, she made me give them back), I had even less time for it. My mum once took me to have my hair cut there and it was so expensive she cut my hair herself from that moment on. The crooked fringes my sister and I sport in our prep school photographs are testament to this.

Meanwhile, in London the scene was set for a more approachable and affordable shopping experience, the like of which had never been seen before.

In the pre-AIDS world of the seventies, dressing up was fun and uninhibited and designers were taking risks. They were becoming personalities in their own right as they collaborated with the up-and-coming stars of the day. Ossie Clark (himself immortalised in David Hockney's famous painting *Mr and Mrs Clark and Percy*) invited Manolo Blahnik to design a shoe collection for his couture collection and Blahnik, who up until 1972 had focused only on designing men's shoes, consequently became the first man to appear on the cover of British *Vogue*. Halston, Zandra Rhodes and Barbara Hulanicki were fast becoming influential in young fashion. My mum says that the department store Biba set up by Hulanicki on London's Kensington Church Street in 1966 was *the* shopping destination. By 1971 Biba had relocated the original shop to a far bigger site. Biba was seven floors of beautiful things, fabulous clothes at prices young people could afford. It hosted exhibitions, played loud music with occasional live bands and had communal changing rooms, something of a novelty back then.

Mum's friend Sue remembers buying a dark blue dress in the new 'midi' length. An actress in the West End, she hadn't bought the dress with anything specific in mind. 'It had a high neck and was made of a woolly jersey fabric with lamb chop sleeves which were very tight at the wrist.' Sue ended up wearing her Biba number with knee-high boots for her 1973 wedding to her husband Roger. Unfortunately, she no longer has the dress. 'Weirdly I don't have any photos, except for a head shot taken in the Baker Street tube station photo booth.' So effortlessly cool, so 1970s.

Jacquie, another family friend, not only has photos of her Biba purchases, she still has them safely stored away. She describes many pieces, but the one that stands out is a pair of lime green bell-bottoms. 'I wore them with a cropped top that showed my midriff and a matching headband. I used to take my three daughters [all under five] to the playground dressed like that.'

Jacquie talks about all manner of fabulous-sounding garments she bought at Biba: kaftans, suede trousersuits and platform sandals. Does she remember what the customer service was like at Biba, did the staff help her to pick out stuff? 'Oh no!' Jacquie laughs. 'The staff didn't help you, it was more like a bazaar, you picked out your own bits and pieces.'

The interior of Biba was like an ocean liner with its sumptuous décor taking inspiration from the Art Deco period. Yet another nursing friend of my mum's, Mary, frequented Biba in a professional capacity where she was employed to look after customers' children while they shopped, one of whom was Barbara Hulanicki's own baby. Your own personal in-store nursery nurse – how very ahead of the game.

Customers headed to Biba to buy something they had spotted on the telly that week, more often than not on the *Ready Steady Go!* presenter Cathy McGowan. McGowan was catapulted to fame when she stumbled into the job of presenter on the Friday night show, which had the slogan 'The weekend starts here'. She was introduced to the Biba designs during a double-page shoot for *Honey* magazine and continued to wear it regularly on the show, which played host to the Beatles and the Rolling Stones. McGowan even collaborated on a collection for Biba.

If Top Shop's flagship store in Oxford Circus is representative of a young brash London today, then in the early seventies Biba marked the turning of the tide in fashion retail with everyone from Julie Christie to Twiggy wearing the label. Sadly, however, by 1975 after a disagreement with the board about creative control, Barbara Hulanicki left the company and not long after Biba's doors closed for the final time.

By the late seventies I had started at my all girls' school in Wimbledon and I had a definite idea of how I wanted to be dressed. We weren't as obsessed with pink as little girls seem to be nowadays, but I did look longingly at bikes that had pastel-coloured ribbons hanging off the handlebars. My dad scoffed at such frivolity; he wouldn't allow stabilisers either. While Dad was usually happy to listen to an argument rather than dismissing it out of hand, he resolutely put his foot down over stabilisers.

My increasing girlyness was perhaps a reaction to the tomboyish outfits that found their way into my wardrobe. There were a lot of boy cousins in our extended family and we had been handed down many of their clothes. My dad's older sister Judith had impeccable taste and dressed her children in beautiful clothes. Breton tops and the softest sweaters bearing French labels were kept carefully in a drawer until I was big enough to wear them. My mum marvelled at the expensive fabrics and the superior quality, but it was lost on me. Even the immaculate cowboy-style tan suede jacket owned by Maggie Smith's younger son Toby Stephens (best known as the Bond villain in *Die Another Day*) ended up in our house. It was when faced with a classroom full of little girls with ponytails that I realised I'd outgrown my cousins' jeans and T-shirts. I didn't want to be mistaken for a boy with my short hair and swimming trunks any more. The fantastic cowboy jacket remained unworn and was handed back to Toby Stephens for his own young children.

My mum bought or made my clothes from then on, but where my sister Hannah didn't care what she wore as long as it wasn't itchy, I wasn't so easy to please. I preferred to shop with my mum and, unusually for a child, I enjoyed it – as long as we weren't shopping for school shoes, which reduced me to tears every time. Luckily my mum had good taste and was pretty handy with a sewing machine. When, in the early hours of Christmas Day 1978, my baby brother arrived, both my sister Hannah and I went to visit him in Kingston hospital in long party dresses with pinafores (very *Downton Abbey*) made entirely by my mum. I had my new Abba annual with me, a gift from a favourite babysitter, and my dad brought along his newly purchased Polaroid camera so he could take some instant photos. That was the seventies I remember – cool, exciting, the start of everything.

CHAPTER TWO

The Levi 501s

Was there any better decade in which to be a teenager than the 1980s, with its loud, brash styles and outspoken spiky-haired role models? While the first half of the seventies was largely a continuation of the romantic and dreamy fashion of the sixties, the second half was a gradual development into those trends famously associated with the eighties. The late seventies had seen a move towards a more expensive, ostentatious aesthetic reflective of a far more money-fixated and image-conscious time. The eighties became synonymous with clothes in vivid shades and very structured shapes, with the angular cut of a padded shoulder and a huge looming hairstyle that helped women feel empowered. In the eighties, women meant business. Working women carried their office footwear in their power handbags allowing them the freedom to walk briskly to work in their trainers.

With the start of the senior school aged eleven came a new school uniform – no more brown lace-ups, bring on the black slip-ons! But the assistant in Russell & Bromley had other ideas. Having measured my feet she told my mum I had fallen arches. The black slip-ons went on the back-burner, I went home with a pair of very expensive navy-blue Kickers, laced up and clumpy. I was utterly crushed. Mum said they were cool and I'd be starting a new trend and everyone at school would be jealous.

It was a nice try, but nobody at school was jealous of my Kickers.

In 1983, a young Madonna and her outspoken take on girl power was the cause of parents' concern. And where Madonna went with her wardrobe, I followed. Madonna was styled by New Yorker Steven Sprouse, who had also worked with my other idol Debbie Harry. It wasn't difficult to reproduce a home version of Madonna's look. Fingerless gloves, ripped lace and masses of neon bangles and necklaces could be bought for under a tenner in one trip to the Monday morning market in the Fairfield car park in Kingston. If my parents minded their eldest child dressing up (or down) in outfits uncomfortably close to those of a prostitute, they never breathed a word to me. We fell out over my constant whining to be allowed to have my ears pierced, but that was about it.

'When can I have my ears pierced then, *when*?' I would demand.

Mum's answer was always the same: 'When you're eighteen. If God had wanted us to have holes in our ear lobes, we'd be born with them.'

This gives the wrong impression of my mum who in fact has little or no belief in any god.

As one friend after another came into school with newly pierced ears, my complaints against my mum increased. 'She'll give in eventually!' those with earrings would insist.

But I knew she wouldn't.

'I can *get married* when I'm sixteen!' I'd wail in a last-ditch attempt to make my mum see how ridiculous she was being. 'I can get married and *leave home* if I want when I'm sixteen – it doesn't make sense that I'm not allowed to do all that with earrings in!'

'Buy some clip-ons then.'

Clip-on earrings, the acceptable face of torture. Painful, ugly and often impossible to keep in place, there wasn't a clip-on earring in Kingston I hadn't attempted to pass off as the genuine article. I found them humiliating, but I found juicy untouched lobes more so.

Then one day somebody invented the tiny shiny 3-D

sticker. For not much more than a pair of plastic 'lozenges' (as my grandfather referred to them once, cementing my despair for good) from Books, Bits and Bobs, the fancy dress and poster shop by the railway bridge, you could buy a whole sheet of the things. Peel 'em off, stick 'em on, you were good to go. It was an enormous breakthrough and from that moment on I was never without stickers on my ears. The only trouble was, my mum then got into them. If ever there was any doubt in her mind about the necessity for ears being pierced (there wasn't) this drew a line under it.

One day when I was thirteen, Mum and I were walking through Bentalls department store when we saw a promotional board for ear piercing declaring: 'Two Is New!'

My mum hadn't even had her ears pierced once – the miniskirts relegated to the closet once us kids came along, she was a jeans-and-jumper-type dresser and it had never occurred to her – but at this moment the idea of having two lots of holes in each ear seemed great fun. Certainly, the poster's smiling tanned beauty with the wind in her hair looked extremely pleased with herself. My first thought was that this unexpected twist in the saga of me getting my ears pierced was the most insensitivity my mum had ever shown me, and it could possibly ruin my life altogether. The second thought that very quickly overshadowed the first was that actually this could change everything. This was my big chance.

We were invited to sit ourselves down in the bright white room tucked away in the Bentalls beauty salon.

The very nice lady in the white coat and excruciatingly tight, shiny bun talked us through the procedure and the aftercare regime and then it was time to get piercing. Out came the little gun.

'Ooo, ow, that hurts, is that it, are we all done?' pleaded Mum, looking at me hopefully. I almost felt sorry for her.

'Erm, no, actually. That was just me drawing the dots on your ears with a pen . . . are you okay for me to carry on?' replied the therapist, now looking slightly anxious.

When the little gold studs were finally in place I knew this was my moment. With my face inches away from my mum's reddening little lobe, I whispered, 'If you don't promise me here and now that I will be allowed to have my ears pierced on my next birthday, I'm going to flick your ear.'

I know. To my own mother. Pure evil. Needless to say, my mum agreed and in March 1986 I got the holes in my ears I (but apparently not God) so desperately wanted. I don't think I have ever wanted anything so much in my life. I didn't feel as if I could go on without pierced ears.

It was a battle hard fought, but it brought me one step closer to being Madonna. Although Madonna had multiple piercings, I was quite happy with my single holes. When aged sixteen I yearned for a second hole and my mum said no, I went ahead and did it anyway. I went to a little studenty boutique called Brilliant hidden around the back of Kingston town centre and hid it from my mum by removing the earring whenever I was at home. After a while it became horribly painful and septic, which was when my mum spotted it. There was a huge row and she made me take it out.

In those pre-mobile phone days, any pictures we took – and we did constantly of ourselves semi-clad in an attempt to replicate our idols – were on our parents' cameras. By the time the photographs had been developed we'd moved on to the next thing. No Photoshop, no Facebook sharing and far fewer eating disorders, or so it seemed. We worried about our skin and the size of our thighs – we were pubescent teenagers poring over *Just 17* and *Mizz* after all – but the diets we experimented with were short-lived, daft and usually based upon Ryvita and cottage cheese. The magazines we read were far more obsessed with how to blend blue and pink eye shadow and what to do with boys than anything else. Or perhaps being a late developer, I simply wasn't that bothered. There was Madonna and Cyndi Lauper, girls just wanting to have fun, and then, on the more serious side, there was Princess Diana. It wasn't much of a choice, even if one of them was a real live princess.

When it came to boys, my crushes were Rob Lowe, Morten Harket of A-ha, Michael J. Fox and Matt Dillon, while George Michael, Rupert Everett and Tom Cruise were among the more popular pin-ups in the class. It wasn't long before *Just 17* launched their own model competition, voted for by post by the readers and awarded with a *Just 17* cover and loads of clothes. Thankfully I was never deluded enough to think I might be model material (despite still being hell-bent on being on the stage) but that didn't stop me falling hook, line and sinker for male-model Steve Wells, the winner of the first ever *Just 17* male-model competition.

Steve, a Surrey schoolboy with a dreamy combination of Indian and Norwegian genes – a 'bit of a dish', according to my mother, with his dark hair, tanned skin and pale eyes – was entered into the competition by his mother. He unsurprisingly made the final round when photographs appeared in the magazine for the public vote, all bomber jackets and baggy pale-blue jeans. We pored over the issue making our predictions and sharing our preferences, and I declared that I simply had to marry Steve Wells.

The Levi's adverts had a lot to answer for. The steady stream of dark and brooding yet clean-cut young men taking off their Levi's jeans to a backdrop of classic tunes such as 'Stand By Me', 'When A Man Loves a Woman' and '20th Century Boy', launched the careers of Nick Kamen and Mario Sorrenti and ensured we all ran out and bought Levi's. Job done. Steve Wells fitted right in. I voted for him and clearly many others did too as a few weeks later he was announced as the winner. I was thrilled and felt I had played my part in his success.

From then on Steve's modelling career had him popping up in magazines as well as the Freeman's catalogue (a fixture in every household) and adverts. What really hammered it home that Steve was slipping from my grasp was when he was pictured with fellow model Terri Seymour on his arm after they met on the set of a shoot for Häagen Dazs ice-cream. Willowy Terri with her abundance of black curls, pearly white grin and endless legs was on another level. Steve Wells may have grown up in Surrey and achieved fame and fortune, thanks to me, but he was no more available to me than Rob Lowe.

Then along came *Neighbours*, which was shown five times a week. The nation was transfixed. Even the accents caught on with a generation of teens irritating their parents with relentless upward inflections at the end of their sentences. My sister Hannah instantly fell for Jason Donovan in his high-waisted jeans and tucked in T-shirt, while Kylie Minogue's character Charlene's questionable apprentice-mechanic style travelled all the way around the world, landing frizzy perms, dungarees and huge hoop earrings on our shores. It is arguable if even the petite and perky Kylie carried off this look, those of us a few stone heavier and without the tan absolutely did not.

Scott and Charlene's love story had us glued to our screens. Simultaneously, the 'Jason and Kylie – are they or aren't they?' story ran and ran. My dad, who had been appointed editor of the *Daily Mirror* by the new owner Robert Maxwell, was delighted to capture the attention of a far younger audience than usual when the real-life romance we'd all hoped was true, was confirmed by the two young actors in an exclusive interview. He remained tight-lipped about what Kylie and Jason had revealed so that Hannah and I didn't discover the answer to the question on everyone's lips until the *Mirror* was on our kitchen table.

At the age of fourteen, I got my first weekend job. Wimbles gift shop in Wimbledon Village was owned and run by my schoolfriend Fleur Greenwood's mum Marie. It was a gorgeous shop that smelt divine and during the tennis tournament fortnight it was the go-to place for tourists looking for tasteful, quintessentially English bits and pieces to take home. Fleur and I would spend our Sundays refilling the potpourri baskets and breaking up tablets of fudge into bags with handwritten labels that we secured with ribbon. It was those bags of fudge that were to be our excuse, should we be confronted, for being open to the public on Sundays, then still against the law. It was impossible not to scoff the odd piece of fudge, although not I hope to the detriment of the day's profits.

I loved working in that shop and, quite apart from fulfilling a lifelong ambition to use a till, it paid me cash in hand which was money to spend at the weekends that I didn't have to ask my dad for. I loved being a small part of the rarefied atmosphere of a small but stylish London enclave. I couldn't afford any of the clothes in the neighbouring boutiques – and neither would I have wanted them at that point – but it was something to aspire to. It was a very different world from my one in Kingston, where our two cats expected to sit up at the kitchen table with the five of us at mealtimes and the running joke was to see who would sit on a strategically placed pea first without noticing. The Wimbledon ladies who lunched were almost from another planet, in their silk and cashmere and their concerns about dog poo and teenagers snogging on the common.

Turning sixteen and being able to apply for a job was something we looked forward to, along with no longer having to wear school uniform and being allowed out of school at lunchtime, which gave us a little taste of freedom and independence. At least two of the girls in my class worked at the local independent shoe shop in Wimbledon Broadway. It was well known that the unwritten part of the job spec was an occasional grope at the top of a ladder in the stock room at the hands of the shop's owner and manager. Beyond giggling about it at school on Monday, it was accepted as just one of those things, the manager a dirty old man to be tolerated. A weekend job made shopping trips and, after a year or so, holidays without our parents, possible.

The latter half of the 1980s was when the boys, the parties and the shopping really took hold. Madonna had met and married bad-boy actor Sean Penn and her single 'Papa Don't Preach' about a teenage pregnancy was about as risqué as it got. The video featured a slightly more demure look for Madonna who was sporting a gamine cropped haircut and, in keeping with the song's character, was dressed in a Breton top and faded, tightly belted Levi's. It was another achievable look for those of us who followed her every move. If 1986 revealed a more grown-up Madonna, though she was still only twenty-seven years of age, in 1989 Madonna and Sean Penn divorced amidst rumours of domestic violence, and the singer moved on to a new romance and yet another new look.

My social life started with a bang at a Gatecrasher ball. The Gatecrasher craze was short-lived and ended as suddenly as it appeared to start. The brainchild of twenty-year-olds Eddie Davenport and Jeremy Taylor, the balls were aimed at teenagers at single-sex public schools who didn't get out much but could afford the expensive £14 ticket. I went to three Gatecrasher balls in all, my first in a marquee in Battersea Park. I borrowed my mum's long red puff-sleeved Laura Ashley gown and wore it with black fishnet tights and my white stilettos dyed black for the occasion. I managed to put my heel through the hem of my mum's dress that evening – I forget the excuse I gave. For the next ball I decided to invest in my own dress. Although the Laura Ashley number was lovely, I wanted something a little more like those frocks I'd spotted on the other Gatecrasher attendees, something shorter, perhaps a bit less covered up, something more me.

I headed alone for Knightsbridge – a strange choice for a skint teenager, perhaps someone said it was good for eveningwear. However, as luck would have it, there was a branch of Warehouse opposite Harrods and it was there that I fell in love for the first time. The dress was little, black and slightly frou-frou, and I knew on sight that it was the one. I felt like a flower fairy in it and didn't want to ever take it off. It was £29.99, a big outlay for a sixteen-year-old in 1988.

In buying that dress I was to learn the all-important lesson of the Cost Per Wear (CPW) theory. Usually reserved for the expensive winter coat or practical black boot, the CPW is the price of a piece of clothing divided by the number of times you wear it. If you keep said item over a number of decades so it gains vintage status, as with the Warehouse dress, you get bonus fashionista points. It is an excellent argument to have at your disposal if ever you feel obliged to explain an expensive purchase to a third person.

Example.

1 x Warehouse LBD bought in 1986: £29.99

Divided by 2 x balls + 1 x office party + 1x eighties costume party

CPW in 2015 = £7.48 (This amount reduces over time with continued usage.)

By the time I went to my next Gatecrasher ball, this time at the Hammersmith Palais, the press had got a whiff of a story. When the pictures of drunken teenagers '*en flagrante*' were splashed all over the papers (including my dad's paper, the *Mirror*) alongside claims this public-school debauchery included alcohol- and drug-induced vomiting and sex under tables, the majority of my class-mates were banned from attending any further balls by their horrified parents. Meanwhile, my own fairly strict dad, who was largely responsible for the story breaking in the first place, said he trusted I wouldn't let myself or him down in this manner and therefore saw no need to ban me. He surprised me often like that, my dad, by being almost unbelievably reasonable. It didn't gain me any friends at school, I hasten to add, and even if I had wanted to go to any further balls, there was nobody left to go with. The balls didn't last long after that, however, and by 1991 Davenport was serving a two-week prison sentence for tax evasion.

The UK was in recession when we left school for the last time in 1990 and therefore finding a full-time job wasn't as easy as I'd imagined. During my gap year, I went to several dreadful interviews for depressingly dull jobs. At one interview for a cash register company in Wimbledon Chase, I remember the interviewer himself suggesting I might be bored working in such an environment and should perhaps look further afield. It was good advice.

I eventually landed a plum job as a receptionist at Vidal Sassoon in Knightsbridge, a stone's throw from

Harvey Nichols. I loved seeing what exciting window would appear next as I walked past on my way to work and sometimes I even dared to have a mooch around the fabulously glossy make-up hall in my lunch hour.

Vidal Sassoon was a lively young place to work and I enjoyed the bitchy campness of it all. The characters there were huge and the drama that could be created in the flick of a comb was quite unlike anything I had seen before. When they weren't plying their trade creating amazing looks on the shop floor – and they were all incredibly good – they were in the staff room having a fag and a coffee, putting the world to rights. They partied hard, those Sassoon stylists. True, they were mostly under thirty, but boy did they work hard, seeing at least eight clients a day, inevitably on their feet all day, grabbing five-minute breaks where they could. I was in awe of them, particularly those who managed to do the whole shift standing in heels. It was a high-fashion environment to be in and not just because of the haircuts. The stylists had their fingers on the pulse and whenever one of them would show up to work in a slightly unusual piece, something by someone I'd never heard of, it would gradually become the next big thing. Obviously, the staff had great hair and were always experimenting with new styles and shades and in that respect I was completely out of my depth with my slightly frizzy bob, which I had intended to look like Madonna's in her 'Express Yourself' video.

One day the assistant manager asked me to see her. 'Emily, can I have a word?'

Who doesn't flinch when they hear those words? I instinctively feel guilty and want to be sick.

The assistant manager, who called herself Regan (there were lots of made-up names there, none of the stylists were just Jane or Bob), was a serene type with the signature Sassoon blunt bob and a sharply cut trouser suit. I found her intimidating enough but when she sat me down in the dark poky office in the basement, our knees touching as we sat side by side at the manager's desk, I was petrified. Was I going to be fired? What had I done? Had I spent too long on a private phone call?

Regan smiled a syrupy smile, utterly without warmth, and told me they thought I didn't look groomed enough and that I needed to wear more make-up. I nearly passed out with the shame. I had worn make-up for years because with my fair colouring I knew I looked better with 'a bit of definition' as my mum, also a fair-skinned blonde, put it. I considered myself ahead of the game in this respect and had always put quite a lot of thought into my appearance so this was a real kick in the teeth. She was absolutely right though: after all, this was Vidal Sassoon and as an eighteen-year-old fresh out of school and drinking cider on the common at weekends, my look was probably more Kingston than Knightsbridge. I upped my game from that day forward and picked up fashion tips from the stylists who, even when they looked scruffy, at least looked designer label scruffy. At that time there weren't too many affordable high-street shops in Knightsbridge so I asked for a pair of shockingly expensive but fabulous shiny Wolford tights for Christmas (copied from the two other receptionists, both called Lisa, one known as Reo) and bought myself my first pair of platform boots (copied off the Lisa still known as Lisa).

And thank goodness I was making a bit more of an effort because on one frosty morning, four years after I put a tick next to his name, *Just 17* model Steve Wells walked in. He was quietly spoken and seemed quite shy, or even embarrassed. I didn't know what to do with myself, I wished I was a stone lighter and regretted putting on my very unforgiving white Levi's that morning. I'd felt quite confident in that day's outfit when I left the house but now Steve Wells was standing in front of me, I felt fat and a bit crap.

When he next approached the counter after he'd had his hair cut, I hit the deck and stayed there under the counter on my knees until he'd gone – my one opportunity to marry him had gone for ever.

I emerged from the floor, brushed off the clumps of hair and dust from my white jeans, now looking rather grubby and strained, to see Steve amble up towards Harvey Nichols (was I trying to console myself, or did he have a funny walk?). That was another lesson learnt: always feel good in what you're wearing, you never know who you might want to impress along the way.

Vidal Sassoon was full of incredibly talented and creative people who were qualified in their chosen career by the time they were twenty years old. I had yet to even start my own training in my chosen career. I felt jealous of their skills which they made look so easy that by the time I left I was convinced I could cut a razor sharp do myself.

I was transferred to the Covent Garden branch. I preferred it there – it was smaller and more intimate and the staff were friendly and kind. There were more fashionable shops for me to shop in too. The money the stylists were earning enabled them to shop in the more high-end shops in the area, the first Ted Baker (in those days selling only shirts) was on Floral Street right opposite our salon, along with Nicole Farhi and Paul Smith. Although it was an introduction to quality brands, I spent most lunchtimes in Neal Street where there was an eclectic mix of cheap market-type goods. My full-time wage was a huge novelty that didn't really wear off for the duration of my stint at Vidal Sassoon, despite the idea being for me to save up for a trip around the States. I appreciated for the first time the freedom that my decent education afforded me, along with the confidence to dream about doing all manner of different things. During my time there I discovered I had won a place at drama school, the Academy of Live and Recorded Arts in south-west London. I couldn't quite believe it as I handed in my notice saying I was off to train to be an actress.

I enjoyed working in a cool and edgy environment where I came face to face with all sorts of interesting people. Designers Mary Quant and Katharine Hamnett (who came in for colour only and would sit there with a pair of scissors snipping away at her own split ends), pop singer Yazz, Victoria Wood and numerous actors visited regularly, and days went quickly. However, I wasn't used to combining being a working girl in central London with my student social life, which intensified when older friends returned home from university and wanted to stay out all hours.

There were two student nights in Kingston, one at Options on a Monday and the other at Ritzy on a Wednesday. I would rush home from work, change into whatever garment I had bought in Covent Garden that day, and rush back out to meet my friends. I had split from my boyfriend of a year and had taken up with his best friend. Cringe. That sort of thing seemed to happen a lot back then, and unbeknown to me my ex was carrying on with my oldest friend too, so perhaps the two cancelled each other out. Is this how all eighteen-year-olds behave? This new love interest, Rupert was his name, wasn't especially interested in me but I was fascinated by him, his cool disinterest and slightly mocking demeanour was probably what reeled me in. Why do we fall for that?

After one night out clubbing, we had returned to my parents' house in the early hours. We stayed up chatting until 7 a.m. when my dad, always an early and enthusiastic riser who genuinely couldn't wait to start each day, came bouncing through the door in his dressing gown. We were sitting on the floor, boots removed but still in our coats and when my dad asked what time I had to be at work I replied, 'Are you joking? I'm not going to work today, I haven't had any sleep!'

My dad laughed, held open the door, pointed to the stairs and said, 'Oh yes you are, go and get ready. It's your stupid fault for not having any sleep, not theirs!'

Rupert all the while sat there, in his coat, staring at the floor, silently dying of embarrassment. I knew at that moment I would be highly unlikely to be able to lure him back to my parents' house again.

Back at school in the late eighties and with most of us doing a weekend job, we had extra cash and with that came the weekend shopping trips. One by one we gained and lost boyfriends and weight, celebrated our eighteenth birthdays and leaving school for good, throwing parties when our parents went away. Weekends without a party to plan for involved a visit to the dark and musty smelling vintage shop American Classics on the King's Road, where hours could be wasted trying on second-hand ripped Levi 501s and oversized T-shirts before lunch at Ed's Diner.

For all the thousands of pounds spent on the Levi adverts, the only thing to be seen in was a pair of already well-worn-in men's faded 501s, preferably with the red line on the inside of the seam to show they were originals. The faded worn-in look had become popular thanks to pop stars such as twins Matt and Luke Goss of Bros and Kylie Minogue, and back then was mostly achieved through genuine wear and tear so vintage was the only way to go unless you wanted to get busy with a pumice stone. My mum was slightly horrified by the amount I spent on jeans that were falling apart and 'didn't even look clean' but that was the look we were after.

Suffice it to say, I wasn't terribly thrilled when one Saturday having spent hours trying and testing piles of jeans in the tiny cubicle downstairs at American Classics, mostly with my back to the mirror, twisted uncomfortably around so I could see my bum, I got my precious 'new' jeans home to find they were far too short in the leg. I hadn't even thought to check the length, so preoccupied were we with the size of our backsides. I wore the jeans anyway, rolled up, pirate style, no 'no quibble refunds' in those days, certainly not for grubby second-hand Levi's anyway.

Not so far from the rather posh King's Road, Kensington market in Kensington High Street was a more edgy shopping destination for punky hair products, lurid-coloured tights and gothicky make-up. I felt rather intimidated by the gloomily lit market that smelt of incense, and was drawn more to the wonderful Hyper Hyper over the road. Hyper Hyper was a spacious bright haven for new young designers and the first home to shoe brand Office London, which opened there in 1981 before its first stand-alone stores opening in 1984 on the King's Road and Charing Cross Road.

Sean Farrell was operations director at Office London when it opened. A charming, dark, well-dressed Irish man with many friends and two identikit wise-cracking younger brothers, Sean remembers they used friends of friends to carry out visits to test the staff at their Office branches. Richard Wharton helped set up the small shop space in Hyper Hyper. In an interview with *Drapers'* magazine in April 2013 he recalled he was given £200 to fit it out. He did so with second-hand furniture: a desk, a swivel chair and a hat stand. Someone commented that it looked more like an office than a shoe shop and the rest is history. In spite of his lack of formal training or experience in footwear, Wharton bought up a load of girls' hockey boots at a snip and then branded them up to sell in Office as fashion must-haves. The 'hockey' boots, considerably marked up, walked off the shelves. Sean adds, 'We also did a Converse All Star rip-off around the same time, we sold thousands of those.' There isn't much Sean doesn't know about footwear, I could talk to him for hours on the subject – we share a hatred of Crocs which shouldn't be a reason to feel you can trust someone, but sort of is in my book.

Hyper Hyper was mostly beyond my budget but it was cool and different and I could happily spend hours just browsing. I was incredibly jealous when my mum bought my sister a gorgeous white sparkly Vicky Martin column dress there to wear at our joint eighteenth and twenty-first birthday party. I wasn't too hard done by, mind you, as my outfit included a pair of cartoonish black suede platform shoes from Sacha specially for the occasion. They were £80 – a huge amount at that time.

Both High Street Kensington and the King's Road were far more idiosyncratic than they are today, with lots of one-off boutiques, risk-taking outlets often very intimidating to a teenager worried about the size of her bottom.

Rupert's older sister Jessica, on the other hand, felt right at home in this salubrious area of west London, working as a Saturday girl at the exclusive Joseph on the King's Road in 1984. As a teenager still at school, she would save up so she could buy pieces in the more high-end shops such as Whistles and Jigsaw, rather than those outlets that tended to be favoured by schoolgirls of the day, the Dorothy Perkins, Miss Selfridge and Top Shops of the high street. Having saved up for a Katharine Hamnett denim skirt from Joseph, Jess then applied for and won her first weekend job there, meeting Joseph himself. Moroccan born Joseph Ettedgui opened this first shop attached to a hairdresser's in 1972 and was the first to bring Prada to London. Within years he stocked Galliano and Jean Paul Gaultier alongside his own-brand basics. While British designer Katharine Hamnett was making her name with crumpled cotton and silk oversized T-shirts emblazoned with political slogans, the Joseph hallmark was a rather more sleek silhouette with the beautifully cut Joseph trouser becoming a 'must-have' piece.

'I spent most of my time standing around being useless, serving the odd customer and "tidying rails",' recalls Jess. 'I wasn't on commission and the full-time girls were. I wasn't encouraged to sell, so I watched. A lot of money was spent on ghastly things which looked ridiculous on the customers, bit of a rip-off really.' A dream job for a teenager, hanging around expensive clothes? Jess, an articulate woman who went on to become a lawyer says, 'I don't think I wanted any of the clothes we sold, some of the stuff was a bit extreme.'

On entering the sixth form Jess left Joseph and landed a job at Scotch House and then Burberry in Knightsbridge, where being on commission she found herself earning a decent amount of money. This fed her love of more expensive clothes.

'I had a really stiff uniform at Burberry and served lots of Japanese and Arab tourists. I sold a lot and made much more cash. It was way before Burberry was trendy but the raincoats were classy, popular and expensive – some had cashmere linings and if you could sell one of those you were laughing.'

Unlike Jess, whose west London posse was far more sophisticated than the Wimbledon one I was a part of, I was a devotee of the high street. The choice was nothing like it is today and proper shopping trips were becoming a weekend pastime. We'd hop on the tube to Oxford

Circus and carefully do a circuit of Top Shop, back then just the one lower-ground floor of ladies wear, and gather armfuls of stuff to try on together. The changing rooms would be full of teenagers throwing clothes from one to the other, laughing and screeching. The less enthusiastic friends were slumped in the corner fully clothed and guarding all the bags, stealing surreptitious glances at strangers in their pants, observers only through a pathological fear of revealing any flesh in this very public arena, our developed bodies still a fascinating novelty. All the physical signs of womanhood were in evidence, but the adult thought processes were some way off.

CHAPTER THREE

The Sweatshirt with the Cut-off Collar

University beckoned. One by one, while I was doing my gap year, my friends left London for pastures new and I found it gut-wrenching. Although I was thrilled to have been offered a place on my first attempt at an accredited drama school (no mean feat as the number of female applicants is always far higher than male), I would be staying in London, and being here without my beloved friends was unthinkable. However, despite this being a good few years before the wonder of mobile phones or social media, we kept in remarkably close contact, I even received the occasional letter from one or two of the boys. We girls had a book which we took it in turns to write in, sending it from person to person. It didn't work quite as efficiently as I had hoped:

'Who has The Book?'

'Does Mandy have The Book, has anyone heard from her?'

'Who has it next, Sara hasn't had it yet?'

'Why haven't I had The Book since last month?'

'Shall I keep it till Christmas and give it to Hannah then?'

When it worked, it was hilarious. It is a toe-curling glimpse into the heads of a bunch of nineteen-year-olds who have no idea what is about to hit them:

'Emily's lost weight, the bitch.'

'Yes, I have a boyfriend, I know it's a bit boring of me but it'll be nice for my birthday . . .'

'I saw Rupert last weekend. He was wearing deck shoes and didn't take his coat off all evening.'

'There's a girl in my class who has slept with Seal.'

My interim job at Vidal Sassoon was handy preparation for drama school, as it turned out. I had been at the same school from the age of seven and so the thought of starting somewhere new was terrifying to me. Just the idea of being in a classroom with the opposite sex was a daunting and not altogether welcome prospect. Although I loved being with 'Our Boys' from the school up the road, learning to hold my own and picking up the choicest examples of the English language in the process, I was distracted by them. Any male attention that came my way made me feel very self-conscious about my appearance. In giving up gymnastics and dancing to concentrate on the drama side of things, I went from a little boy shape able to cut a dash in the skinniest of drainpipes and sparkly jumpers to a curvy one in no time at all. It was an uneasy transition for me and suddenly I didn't feel quite so at home prancing about in a leotard or swimming costume. This would prove to be awkward at drama school, those singing and dancing scenes and the kids from *Fame* were not as far from reality as you'd imagine – occasionally during a lunch hour, someone would break out into a song-and-dance routine – as horrific as that must sound to the uninitiated.

I bought the official Academy of Live and Recorded Arts black sweatshirt in the largest size available and cut the neckline and cuffs off so that it looked more like something Legs and Co. would wear on *Top of the Pops*. I could do the dance steps, that wasn't a problem, I just didn't like watching myself in the huge floor-to-ceiling mirrors, which was a new and unwelcome feeling for me. I'd never previously given any thought to how I looked at gymnastics competitions or dance shows. I loved dancing and had been very confident, but suddenly I was the shy girl in the class pulling at the hem of her sweatshirt so as little of my body was on show as possible. Thank goodness for my brilliant new friend Lee who not only didn't care when he couldn't do a step, but without his glasses on couldn't see a reflection anyway, neither mine nor his own. We would stand near the back and giggle uncontrollably – me all frizzy blond hair and billowing sweatshirt, Lee's red face clashing with the second-hand pink Converse boots he rarely took off. We must have looked an odd pair, but Lee's bookish appearance belied his outrageous and cutting wit and I liked him instantly. He was gay so he didn't give two hoots about what my body did or didn't look like and although we were capable of spending whole lunch breaks ogling the dancers who wandered past (I had set my sights on a bloke in the year above who wore dungarees with nothing underneath, therefore far too intimidating for me to ever speak to), more often than not we would be doing impressions of our fellow students or quoting *Wood and Walters*.

In lessons, Lee would sit bolt upright (courtesy of his Alexander Technique training) bored stiff, until suddenly someone would say something ridiculous and Lee, who had appeared to be asleep with his eyes open, would guffaw loudly making everyone jump, and then follow it up with a timely quote from Victoria Wood's *Acorn Antiques*. I had a new pal and, although I couldn't talk fashion with this one, he swore like a trooper and was more than happy to share cake and a gossip, so I soon settled in.

It was around this time that one evening Lee suggested we go to the Fridge club in Brixton to see a new boy-band who were making an appearance. Welcome to the stage a very new, very young and scantily clad Take

That. I didn't bat an eyelid at the dungaree man at college after that.

Like most of those in my year at the Academy of Live and Recorded Arts, I quickly got myself a part-time job to keep the wolf from the door. I had taken a year off after school but was still only nineteen when I started my first year, so the full-time nature of the course wasn't alien to me. Unlike most of the degree courses my school friends were on at university, at drama school we had to report in every day and be there for every class, or else. The boys tended not to be keen on the dance classes – we did ballet, tap, modern and historical dance – and would regularly bunk off. However, ALRA had a strict three strikes and you're out policy, so by the time we graduated we were down to only nine boys and twenty girls. It doesn't take a theatre or film expert to immediately spot the inherent problem this presents in terms of casting. Take any Shakespeare play and look at the list of players, it is at least two-thirds men. Films with good strong female leads are less of a rarity now but there will probably always be more actresses available for fewer roles while for men it's the other way round. It's one of the great injustices of this horribly discriminatory profession but as long as it appeals as a glamorous vocation, young women will be drawn to it.

In the early 1990s when we were immersed in all things thespian, we had some impressively strong role models, like Jodie Foster, who had won two Oscars in the space of three years for two largely unglamorous roles

(*The Accused* and *Silence of the Lambs*); despite growing up in the spotlight, she presented the positive side of women in film, with a healthy attitude to fashion never bowing to any pressure to be something she wasn't. Between 1990 and 1993 there was a run of popular films like *Pretty Woman*, *Basic Instinct*, *Thelma and Louise* and *True Romance*, which were not only great stories capturing the imagination of men and women alike, but the overriding stars were the women rather than the men. Julia Roberts, Sharon Stone, Gina Davis, Susan Sarandon and Patricia Arquette all had praise and award nominations heaped on them. It seemed to be a good time to be a woman in the acting industry, if you weren't too bothered about the finer details of the roles they played. And we weren't. Of course we were aware you needed to be fit and look good in order to have the best chance at a wide range of parts, but we wouldn't let a small thing like gender equality get in the way, we just wanted to be able to work.

My first student job was as a waitress for Pizza Hut in Tooting Broadway near to where I shared a pretty horrible student house. Me, three other acting students and the snails, who only came out at night, but made a terrible mess on the carpet when they did.

The Pizza Hut position was my first waitressing job and I really enjoyed it. There was free pizza on each shift I worked and the assistant manager, who was extremely flirtatious, made the time pass more quickly. Discovering I wasn't the only one he'd propositioned took the shine off the job a little, as did the company's decision to add braces to the red-and-black Pizza Hut uniform. Braces and boobs do not work, in much the same way as long strands of beads don't. I didn't seek revenge on the assistant manager exactly, but I did award myself a few extra perks. As many huge handfuls of toppings on my pizza as took my fancy and then at the end of my shift, as the assistant manager gave me instructions for clearing up, I would stand there listening and nodding, while sipping from the Diet Coke takeaway cup in my hand. A cup full to the brim of the Pizza Hut house white.

My next job was at Ritz video where I polished off almost as many bags of popcorn as I did films. No wonder I had to slim down into the skimpy night dress and bloomers ensemble that made up part of my costume for the first of my third-year plays. Lee and I took to doing regular exercise videos before college and I started to cycle in each morning. Although I told myself I was there to learn, at times I desperately missed the enthusiastic reassurance my dad readily handed out, or the unconditional loyalty you can only find at home. Blaming my looks on anything that went wrong, I felt heavy and ungainly compared to many of the other girls, which I wasn't used to. As the pressure mounted to attract the interest of an agent before we graduated, I became more and more paranoid that I was starting to look like a cartoon blonde. Securing an agent before leaving drama school is almost unheard of, unless you're very lucky indeed, but it became an obsession. Everyone went off and got terribly glam (and not always very true to life) 10 x 8 black-and-white headshots and then spent a fortune sending them out to all and sundry.

My concerns about my 'look' were cruelly confirmed during a class taken by actor director Jeremy Young. Jeremy was a regular teacher at ALRA and like most of the teachers, he taught in between acting jobs. He was once married to the actress Kate O'Mara, something he mentioned often and, interestingly, seemed to be the role of which he was most proud. The purpose of this class was for everyone to bring in their headshots so we could all discuss whether or not it was a good representation. The dreaded 'Photos Class' was almost as infamous as the 'Snogging Class' and the 'Nudity Class'. Those mythical stories supposedly passed down by former students and then shared in the bar, started doing the rounds way before they actually happened, if indeed they happened at all. Legends of students leaving the room in tears and giving up the course for good as a result of the Photos Class put the fear of God in me.

The dreaded day arrived. Jeremy had us lay our photographs out on the floor and we all had a good look at them awaiting the moment when he, as the seasoned professional, would critique them.

'What do we think of Lee's picture, hmm? It's all right. Teeth look funny . . .'

'Sunna looks good doesn't she? Excellent legs but my eye is immediately drawn . . . can I see up her skirt or not?

Heads only everyone, okay? Heads only, unless you want directors asking you in for a different reason.'

Then it was my turn. Jeremy asked the class what they thought. A few allies commented that they thought it was a good likeness and then there was an ominous silence. Jeremy puffed himself up before saying, 'Yes, well, pretty blonde, young, two a penny, lots of hair, nice enough, BUT . . .'

Mr Young then helpfully informed the class that if I was 'seen' for the young romantic lead role for which my face would suggest I might be suitable, I would walk through the door and lose the part as soon as they set eyes on the rest of me.

'Emily either needs to lose weight or gain it, people. Otherwise she's going to be playing barmaid roles. You know Sharon in *EastEnders*? You see? You'll never play Juliet if you're a stone overweight, people. I'm not being mean, I know you think I'm being a wanker but look at me, look at my huge conk, I never played Romeo, not good-looking enough, could do a Laertes, not Romeo, far too old now of course . . .'

I was mortified, as was the rest of the class, I suspect. It was an unkind thing to say to someone so young and clearly not delivered in the most sensitive manner, but in terms of the reality of the profession, Jeremy had a very good point. Drama school tells its students a lot of things they don't particularly want to hear. Many of my fellow students, for example, didn't like being forced to learn how to speak in RP (Received Pronunciation – the 'non-accent' of so-called standard English) so that the Yorkshire/Norwegian/Dorset accent didn't restrict the roles they could go up for. My own battle was flattening out my very London public-school accent. To those few who objected to working on their vowel sounds, my accent was simply considered 'posh', which was exactly what some people thought RP was. This wasn't the case at all and if anything made me feel paranoid about how I spoke, which added to my shyness at the beginning of our course.

Drama school often aims to break its students down into tiny little pieces to then mould them back into strong fine actors who can turn their hand to any role. It's an interesting idea but it doesn't always work. Not everyone is cut out for a life of rejection and unemployment. The highs are so gloriously high you can live off the adrenalin for months. But the lows . . . imagine getting down to the final two for an amazing job, the role of your dreams in fact, a nine-month run in London's West End, a role which has the potential to change your career for ever and then losing out because of your hair colour – they suddenly decided they wanted a brunette. That happened to me and it's not even unusual, frankly it's one of the least hurtful reasons I've failed to get a job.

As harsh as drama school can be, it doesn't prepare you for the harsh reality of the profession, it isn't possible. At first all you want is to get your foot in the door of an audition and everything will take off from there . . . if I can just get my first job . . . how come it's so hard to get a second job . . . and then a third . . . how will I pay my bills if I take this profit share play . . . why do I never get seen for telly jobs . . . if I've been out of acting work for more than six months am I still an actress . . . will I still remember how to do it when the day finally comes . . . You don't discuss any of this stuff when you're actually at drama school, it is the big elephant in the room for the whole three years. Everyone is quietly competing with everyone else. It's not the greatest environment for friendships to grow but amazingly they do. Perhaps there is no coincidence that my greatest friends from this time couldn't be less similar to me physically. It certainly helps if you are never likely to be considered for the same role.

I met my friend Clare at drama school. Born in Harrogate in Yorkshire, she had left home at eighteen to come to London, following in the footsteps of her childhood friend, actor Hugo Speer, who had trained at Arts Educational drama school.

A family friend who was looking out for London-bound Clare suggested she come to work at the General Trading Company where she herself worked as buyer for the Oriental department. The GTC was located in Chelsea's well-to-do Sloane Square and Clare found herself working full-time in the glassware department alongside Santa Palmer Tomkinson, better known as the novelist Santa Montefiore and sister of the infamous Tara. According to

Clare, it was accepted that a job at the GTC was a good way of meeting your future husband. Since you had to physically go to the shop to see a wedding list and research it with your own eyes, the theory was that when the single male friends of the groom came in to browse for a gift, you made yourself indispensable. Forever. A few of the young ladies were like Clare, at the GTC to fill in before going on to university, but many were there until they were scooped up by a handsome prince.

Although Yorkshire-bred Clare had her moments (she was reprimanded for wearing black leather clogs to one shift), she knew how best to dress her tiny size 6 frame and did so with vintage finds. Her look was eclectic and feminine, and she had a knack of looking wonderful and yet you just knew if you asked her about any of her clothes, the response would be 'Oh, this old thing . . . this was 50p in Oxfam.'

Clare happily went along with the assumption made by her colleagues that she had attended Harrogate Ladies College when she had in fact been a pupil at Knaresborough Tech. It was a lovely introduction to London and it was at GTC that she met Joan Collins, the Queen Mother and Rob Lowe shopping for homewares, although disappointingly not as a group.

Clare and I didn't become really good friends until the third year at ALRA. I knew her because she hung out with my housemate Lauren but because we never had the same classes it wasn't until our penultimate term at college that our paths properly crossed. And what a path it was. As I mentioned, by the time we reached the third year, so many of the men had left or been thrown out that casting for the shows must have been a nightmare. They reeled out *The House of Bernarda Alba* and *Don Juan Comes Back From the War*, both sombre affairs made up of mainly female characters, but in the second term they were struggling. Having cast two-thirds of the students, I think they found they were left with a bunch of reprobates they simply didn't know what to do with. So it was decided we would perform an evening of music hall. It was a complete farce from start to finish and not one of us wanted to be in it, but it was possibly the most fun I've ever had.

One student had refused to take part at all, meaning a second-year student had to be drafted in to take his place. This turn of events was scandalous at the time but ultimately worked out to my advantage as I was then partnered with this new boy named James Lee. James and I became great friends and once the principal of ALRA talked him into cutting off his long ponytail, I decided I quite fancied him. He was terribly sensible and wise beyond his nineteen years (and my twenty-one) and suggested we shouldn't get involved until after the show was over. I had never heard such buttoned-up nonsense but I didn't have much choice other than to go along with it. We eventually went out on a date in the Easter holidays before my last term at ALRA.

The music hall evening was directed by Doreen Hermitage, an actress and dancer and regular at London's

Players' Theatre. She would appear at rehearsal each morning immaculate in a pink tracksuit, her white hair scraped back into a bun held by a bright plastic flower. She was never not exasperated by us and our inability to show any sign of talent in this area. A student would take their position onstage to perform their number and, within moments, Doreen would be sighing, raising her eyes to heaven and slapping her hand on her thigh along to the piano accompaniment while shrieking, '*KEEP IN TIME!*'

Mr Barrie Bignold on the piano, whom Doreen insisted on referring to as 'Big Nose', had the patience of a saint. He was a successful musical director so this must have been hell for him, but he suffered in silence, unlike Doreen who made no secret of her desire to be elsewhere.

To be fair to Barrie and Doreen, we behaved like children most of the time. Weeks into the rehearsal process, when the show should have been coming together, we were still mucking about and forgetting lines. Clare and I didn't help matters: on one occasion, throwing our fellow student Jonathan into a blind panic about his performance because the rest of the company, who were seated in the auditorium, were laughing their heads off. As a performer you usually appreciate a loud laugh and you can't help but listen out for it, but in the wrong place it can be devastating. Much to Doreen's irritation, poor Jonathan kept stopping his song, completely paranoid about the hysteria going on around him. Doreen assumed the cast were merely imbeciles for laughing at the idiot on the stage who kept forgetting his lines. Neither Jonathan nor Doreen had a clue that each time he started to sing (beautifully, I might add) Clare and I, who were hidden in the wings, were pushing a giant snowman out to have a good look around the theatre before disappearing back into the wings. It was utterly childish and one of those moments when you seriously believe you may die laughing. Poor Jonathan, I'm not sure he ever saw the funny side.

After the music-hall experience, which amazingly turned out all right and I conquered my fear of singing solo, Clare and I were firm friends. Physically we are polar opposites – she's little and always looked cute, even as a student, while I really didn't. I tried to pick up tips from Clare about how to spot the good second-hand stuff, but the grunge look that was so in during our time at drama school simply didn't do my curves any favours. Clare is a frequent and clever shopper who is drawn to colour and has an eye for vintage style, I am a fashion victim through and through. Where Clare could pick out a fur coat and a green scarf to throw over a Liberty print dress and cropped mohair cardigan and look every inch the London actress, I would look more like a moth-eaten bag lady who had swallowed Helena Bonham Carter. I didn't even particularly like the grunge look, but it was the perfect smokescreen to what I saw as my undesirable and imperfect body beneath. Clare was sanguine about her lack of cleavage and height, whereas I had a long way to go to come to terms with my adult body.

Clare and I were shopaholics. Our shopping trips together became epic. I tend to prefer shopping alone when I can spend frivolously without anyone looking over my shoulder but I made an exception for Clare and always looked forward to our shopping trips. We had the routine down pat so there was rarely the need for anything other than a 'See you at the usual place at 1.30 p.m.' and it was in the diary. To be clear, there was never any lunch involved, we had bigger fish to fry.

Our 'usual place' was Hennes on Oxford Street, right opposite the tube station. We didn't bother with anywhere else because we knew this shop would scratch the itch. As far as we were concerned, it didn't get any better than Hennes on Oxford Street.

'How you doing? How was work?' Clare would ask when I arrived.

'Oh you know, all right, uneventful. You?'

'Same really . . .' answered Clare as she strode across the road, careful not to miss the green man – a missed green man was precious wasted minutes in Hennes. Clare wouldn't dart in between traffic to get across a busy road like I would. She would however happily yell at a motorist she considered to be driving dangerously, even if it was nothing to do with her. She got away with it too as no one ever thought her capable of such a thing: her pretty dresses and petite stature were a cunning disguise.

Once through the huge hallowed doors and into the bright white emporium, three floors of rail upon rail of tempting product, we were under the spell. Hennes was our drug.

What followed was a well-rehearsed cha-cha-cha of one step forward, three steps back – the occasional cross-over where we met in the middle and regular pauses to look in one of the floor-to-ceiling mirrors.

'Did you hear back from that bloke?' called out Clare, a pair of jeans over one shoulder, a shoulder strap of bag between her teeth.

'Which one?' I called back before darting off to the other side of the shop to check something on a mannequin.

Next time I caught up with Clare, she had an olive green jacket on and was holding a blue skirt up to the light, as she said, 'That bloke who told you he would call back when he'd finished fixing his mum's computer?'

'Oh him. No, never did. Yeah well, I had a good cry about it but I'm fine now. Did you get a call back for that telly part?' I asked, as I measured the difference between a size 12 dress and the same dress in a size 14. There didn't seem to be that much difference and, yet, I didn't want to have to buy a size 14 if I could help it. 'Do you think this dress would make me look huge or do you think the sequins might actually distract from the bulk?'

Clare laughed, a throwing-back-her-head, all-encompassing laugh. 'I don't think it would make you look huge, because you're not huge but I do think it would make you look like a prostitute,' she retorted. 'Have I got an olive jacket already? I think I might have one just like this at home . . .'

'I think you bought something very similar to that last time we came here. And you asked me the same thing that time too. I don't really mind looking like a prostitute. I'm going to try it on.'

Clare pulled a face, a mixture of 'whatever' and 'I'd be disappointed if you didn't'.

And so it went on until both of us were so laden down with clothes we had no choice but to head to the fitting rooms, if only for a sit down and a sip of water.

'How many items have you got?' asked the disinterested assistant in charge of the plastic tags.

'I don't know, at least eight,' replied Clare.

'You can only take six items in . . .' said the assistant, a definite hint of triumph in her tone.

'Well can I leave some out here then?' This conversation wasn't going to end well. Clare would have been better off asking the assistant if she could vomit all over the floor.

After a lengthy sigh and what seemed like the slowest movement possible, the assistant counted out six items, which she gave back to Clare along with the appropriate plastic tag.

'The other fifteen items will be out here on the rail,' the assistant said, bored.

I quickly counted up the clothes in my arms and told

the assistant with pride that I only had eleven items. She sucked her teeth, told me she didn't have another 'six' tag and handed me a 'five' and a 'one' instead.

If the assistant thought we were annoying already, it was very lucky she then sloped off to her lunch break leaving Clare and I to flit backwards and forwards between our cubicles and the 'unwanted garments' rail. The next time I looked at my watch, we'd been in there an hour and a half. Clare had tried on all twenty-one pieces of clothing along with a couple of mine. Not the prostitute dress though. I didn't fit in the size 12 after all and having to resort to the size 14 put me off the whole idea: £14.99 saved. I picked out those bits I couldn't live without and hung those I'd decided against on the rail outside.

My tummy rumbled as I made my way to the accessories area to choose some jewellery. Clare soon appeared beside me, a heap of clothes in her arms.

'I'm going to pay now, I haven't any hands free to look at anything else,' and off she went, a long scarf trailing behind her collecting dust and hair from the floor as she went.

At the counter, the assistant laboriously counted out all Clare's stuff into bags and when she was done and the total flashed up onto the till, it was just over £100.

'What? It can't be that much, can you just check . . .' Clare was starting to turn a little red.

'You've bought sixteen items,' stated the assistant, checking a fingernail.

I started to laugh. I could see Clare was itching to say something about the assistant's attitude but was also dividing the total price by sixteen in her head, so in the end she let it go.

Weighed down by the familiar and exciting red-and-white plastic bags, two-and-a-half hours after we'd met up, we kissed each other goodbye and set off for home, exhausted and starving.

The three years at ALRA weren't my most comfortable, I loved learning my craft and I was excited about the road ahead but I felt a little on the outside looking in at drama school. I worked hard and did well there but I was often trying to be something I wasn't; I didn't want to be cast as the funny wise-cracking blousy barmaid but that seemed to be exactly where I was headed. Lee once announced that he thought I would come into my own aged forty. I appreciated the sentiment (some of the best Oscar Wilde roles are the ladies of a certain age), but it's not exactly what you want to hear when you're twenty-one.

On graduating ALRA at the age of twenty-two, and with no agent to represent me, I set about writing off for jobs advertised in *PCR*, a weekly newsletter for actors. If it wasn't for *PCR* (I can't even remember what this stands for) most of us probably wouldn't have had a lifeline to the industry at all. It was full of an unbelievable amount of old tosh and every now and again it would print some unsuspecting casting director's name alongside an item about the new Bond film or something by Richard Curtis. This would prompt every actor in existence, suitable or not, to stuff their photograph, CV and a covering letter in an A4 envelope and send it to the casting director's office or, worse, their house. Amazingly, I did actually win parts, including a Caribbean gig and a run at the King's Head theatre in Islington as a result of *PCR*, but to my knowledge nobody ever became rich and famous because of it.

I called in any contacts I could think of in the quest to get my first acting job and among these was the American theatre director Michael Rudman. Michael, who had taken on the role of artistic director of the Sheffield Crucible theatre after a stint as associate director at the National, knew my dad, and so when I got in touch he very kindly offered me an audition for the title role in his production of *Romeo and Juliet*. Are you thinking what I'm thinking? Well, yes, quite apart from being a bit chubby and completely inexperienced, I was terrified. I didn't get the part, unsurprisingly. (A few years later when I auditioned for Mr Rudman again, he commented on my appearance, 'Emily, gosh, you must be at least two stone lighter than when I last saw you!' and I recalled the excruciating comment from Jeremy Young in that drama class. As I said, he hadn't been that far off the mark.) Michael was also greatly amused upon looking at my contact details that I had a mobile telephone number.

'A young actress with a mobile phone? I've seen it all now!'

It was 1994 and up to this time mobile phones were something only big shots had, not even my dad as editor of a national newspaper had one. For some reason I decided this new technology was an excellent investment and used £150 of my savings for an enormous Mercury one2one handset with a foldable aerial. It was absolutely rubbish by today's standards but the tariff was free calls to landlines between 7 p.m. and 7 a.m. and at weekends. Since nobody else had a mobile phone this was perfect. I undoubtedly got my money's worth with the amount of gassing I did on the phone in the evening to friends.

It's absolutely true there is 'no business like show business', it can be like a drug. But it is a cruel profession and no other industry gets away with the arbitrary nature of the employment it offers. It isn't just about talent, if only it were that simple, it's a combination of luck, timing, what you look like, who you know, and bucketloads of self-belief. Oh, and talent helps long-term. Rarely is just one of these attributes enough.

The first thing I did upon leaving drama school was to move back home to Mum and Dad in Kingston. James and I had been an official item for a few months but he still had another year to go at drama school so he moved in with a friend and I very happily went back to the comforts of my family home. My sister was off to university so there was one less person in the house and after three years of student living it was a joy to be home. The second thing on my list was to get a job. I was not the sort of person who was happy to sit around waiting for the telephone to ring. There are actors who will breezily sign on and then loaf about but that sort of existence would drive me mad. I have to be busy, as busy as possible most of the time. I will even find something to do at 11 p.m. when I'm about to go to bed. I have ants in my pants (what a horrific thought that is) and my mum is the same – my granny used to say Mum was skinny because she never sat still. Likewise, I will have a telephone conversation while applying make-up and eating breakfast. I'm not convinced any of it saves time.

I was lucky enough to get a job for Episode, an up-and-coming fashion brand that happened to be opening a new concession in Dickins and Jones in Richmond. Episode sold lovely feminine tailored pieces in beautiful fabrics, which was just right for the wealthy women of Richmond-upon-Thames. Unfortunately the dyed-in-the-wool assistants of the first floor of Dickins and Jones didn't quite see it that way. As the builders moved in and set about tearing down the dreary old House of Fraser fittings and fixtures to replace them with the far more stylish and modern light-cherry wood ones of the Episode brand, so the middle-aged managers of Jaeger, Country Casuals and Wallis, with their permed bobs, sensible navy shoes and gold jewellery, gathered to spit bullets.

It was a time of change in department stores. At the time, they were seen as dinosaurs that couldn't possibly last. The department-store managements fought back with refurbishments to create a more modern selling space that would appeal to a younger customer. At House of Fraser this involved boarding up all the windows and doing away with natural light. Meanwhile, Selfridges launched a £94-million redevelopment programme and introduced a new yellow carrier bag.

Dickins and Jones had allotted double the usual amount of floor space to Episode, and what with the wood-panelled floor, elegant signage and prime position right at the top of the escalators, we were the enemy before we sales associates (a new label for the humble staff who until then were known as shop assistants) even arrived. Then the stock was wheeled in. Silk suits in muted shades hung heavily on the thick wooden Episode hangers, with piles of folded cashmere sweaters sitting neatly above on polished glass shelves. The large wooden table in the centre of the shop floor featured a tall vase of fresh lilies with velvet scarves and glass necklaces dotted all around. The calm and uncluttered atmosphere of Episode stood out like a sore thumb in among all the old-school department-store fare – things were a-changing in the world of department stores and the stalwarts of Dickins and Jones didn't like it one bit.

But I loved it! It was my first job on the shop floor and although I was never going to set the world on fire with my selling skills (we weren't on commission, thank God), I loved wearing the gorgeous clothes and chatting to customers about them, helping to build outfits for them and occasionally even selling the odd piece. It suited me down to the ground. I was very glad of the flattering tailoring of the clothes that came with the job. People started to comment that I'd lost weight and looked great when it was simply a change from the voluminous garments I'd worn at drama school. Episode introduced me to how a fabulous cut of jacket or trouser can streamline the silhouette and skim pounds off you. I spent a ridiculous amount of time trying on the clothes myself and dressing up the mannequins. I walked around Richmond looking and feeling like a serious professional when actually I was a skint aspiring actress living with her parents, rushing to auditions in between shifts and often struggling horribly with the endless rejection and long periods without an acting job.

A few months in, another part-time vacancy opened up in the Episode concession. Clare was in between jobs and as luck would have it she loved hanging out in shops and trying clothes on just as much as I did. The perfect qualifications! I persuaded her to interview and soon the two of us were working side by side on the shop floor at Episode. If I wasn't getting much work done before, this certainly wasn't going to improve things.

We never knew what we would receive in the weekly stock deliveries and so we would excitedly tear open the boxes so we could try everything on – a necessity for advising customers on cut and sizing, of course – before dressing the mannequins, one of my favourite pastimes. It's only one step up from playing with dolls really.

It was during one of these stock delivery days, a slow weekday afternoon, that Clare was caught out by the mystery shopper. We had been warned by our area manager that at some point over the next few weeks our concession would be visited by someone posing as a shopper. This undercover person would then report back on her findings and we would get feedback from head office. I was fascinated but anxious. I'd heard colleagues at Pizza Hut talking about a similar thing but had never actually come into contact with one of these so-called mystery shoppers. We were intrigued and as trained actresses ourselves tried to imagine what these characters would look like. Would we be able to spot one? Did we imagine this woman to be dressed in dark glasses and a trench coat with a magnifying glass in one hand and a clipboard under her arm? Suffice it to say, neither of us had a clue, and that was how we – or rather, Clare – came unstuck.

We weren't overly bothered at the thought of the mystery shopper in our midst. Clare and I both saw this job as a stop-gap and probably didn't take it as seriously as the management had hoped – whoever had thought it was a good idea to let us work our shifts together was putting a lot of misguided faith in us to behave, let alone do our jobs properly. As the days passed without any sign of anyone even remotely suspicious, we let our guard down. Perhaps the shopper had been already, reported her findings to the area manager and our fate was sealed.

'Oh shit, I bet it was that woman who came in on Thursday,' wailed Clare one morning as I idly poked through the sale rail across the floor in Jaeger. 'The one who was asking if we had any skirts which fell below the knee,' she went on.

'And? What happened?' I asked, only half listening. Customers of a certain age complaining about our skirt lengths being too short were two a penny, I'd heard it all before. Richmond society in general was not overly pleased with Episode's approach to skirt lengths and I was becoming bored of repeating myself.

'I couldn't be bothered to show her any alternatives so I sent her over to Country Casuals . . . it seemed more her sort of thing.' I looked up from the tired-looking knitwear and we both laughed conspiratorially.

'I wouldn't worry about it,' I said. 'After all, one successful audition and we're out of here.'

At that moment a smartly dressed lady approached and started looking at a silk scarf on the mannequin. Clare and I both paused to smile and acknowledge the customer as she continued to browse.

'And talking of being out of here,' I added, 'I'm gasping for a cuppa. I'm going to take my tea break, are you okay to start opening up the new delivery?' I knew this was an unnecessary question. Deliveries were what we lived for at Episode – the excitement of seeing what we'd been sent and the chance to delve in and try it all on was the highlight of any shift, especially one as uneventful as this one. As I wandered off to the staff room, I heard the sound of Clare ripping enthusiastically through the taped box of stock.

When I returned to the department fifteen minutes later, there was no sign of Clare. The curtain was drawn across the fitting-room cubicle so I guessed that she had gone to fetch a piece from the stock room on the other side of the floor. I smiled at the denim-clad customer hanging around the fitting room, assuming she was waiting for the customer within and asked if there was anything I could help her with. Just as the customer opened her mouth to respond, the fitting-room curtain was torn back with a dramatic swoosh and there stood Clare in Hollywood starlet pose, hands on hips, head cocked to one side. 'Ta-daaaa!' she proclaimed as the taken-aback customer and I stared in bewildered awe at her. She was dressed head to toe in new season stock, price tickets swinging from every piece.

I'm sorry to say my improvisation skills failed me the day that Clare was caught by the mystery shopper with her uniform in a pile on the fitting room floor. Of course it wasn't until we were both taken to one side and given a stern talking to by the area manager a fortnight later that we even realised it had happened. It didn't take long for us to laugh it off but unsurprisingly it was the disapproving staff of Jaeger and Country Casuals who had the last laugh. Neither Clare nor I lasted much longer at Episode after that.

CHAPTER FOUR

The White Nylon Trouser Suit

My whole family were so proud when the call came through to say I'd landed the part of Nancy in *The Country Girl*. My dad actually whooped and fist-pumped the air. I would be playing a young actress in her first role with Corin Redgrave and Kika Markham at Greenwich Theatre. I was ecstatic: it was a gift of a part and to be appearing with the Redgraves (Corin and Kika were husband and wife) was more exciting than I could possibly have imagined. My dad immediately fished out Michael Redgrave's biography from his bookshelf so I could get a bit of background on this most famous of acting dynasties. Kika and I were the only women in the cast and so we had a huge dressing room all to ourselves at the theatre while all the boys (seven of them in total) shared one.

The first morning of rehearsal I walked into Greenwich Theatre sick with nerves. I had met the director Annie Castledine once before at the audition and she had been perfectly pleasant, but I knew through the grapevine that she was a force to be reckoned with. Within five minutes of entering the rehearsal room, it became obvious that I was the only member of the cast who didn't know everyone else. I stood there feeling like I was five years old, except far less cute.

'*Use it*, Emily,' Annie bellowed across the big room from where she sat all in black in a low chair in the far corner. 'Remember the feeling you have now and *use it*!'

I don't know how I didn't cry. Except crying would have been unacceptable and this was finally what I'd dreamed of: a professional job, and a bloody good one too.

The very tall Dan Stewart took the third lead role, that of the director in the play. I had a bit of a crush on him and his response was to tease me as he would a younger sister. Even though it was an experience that helped with the characterisation of my role, I wanted to be a proper member of the cast, not just the silly airhead who shouldn't be drinking with the boys in the bar. One day during rehearsal, Annie had Corin and me standing onstage behind a large white gauze screen which she'd had an idea could represent the stage within the play. The rest of the cast sat around, as you do, in the auditorium. When the stage lights came up on the gauze, enormous silhouettes of Corin and me loomed over the whole stage. From the laughter in the cheap seats the vaguely transatlantic voice of Dan Stewart laughed, 'Emily looks absolutely *huge*!'

'Oh Dan, stop it . . .' I heard the kindly Kika scold.

'Well she does, she looks *massive*!' continued Dan.

Corin and I stood there quietly still as directed by Annie, also seated in the stalls. The laughter continued until very slowly I lifted the middle finger of my huge right hand and held it up into the spotlight.

Director Annie's tobacco-edged guffaw rang out. '*Well done, girl!*' My confidence was restored.

When the first night of *The Country Girl* arrived, it was hard to tell who in my family was the most excited about it. Indeed, unbeknown to me, it turned into a competition in the foyer as my mum, dad and brother arrived to discover my uncle David and his girlfriend Karin (by now, David and my aunt Jude had divorced) had arrived over an hour earlier and already purchased enough theatre programmes for everyone in the party. In fact, David and Karin had arrived in Greenwich so early that I had bumped into them in a cafe around the corner during my break before getting into costume. They presented me with a beautiful antique brooch to mark the occasion.

David was a generous man, but also he knew only too well the significance of this night. I was only a year out of drama school but had longed for this day for far longer.

Back in the foyer, my mum, who looked gorgeous in a sleek black Gerard Darel trouser suit she had bought for the occasion, was a bundle of nerves. As a mum, I think perhaps you never get over the nerves you experience when your child is onstage, no matter whether they are in the school nativity or on the West End stage. My dad was calmer. Although, when he discovered he had been pipped to the post at the programme queue by David, Dad obstinately bought even more programmes which he gave to my boyfriend James, drama-school friend Lee and various other friends as they wandered in. Then, when the performance was about to start and everyone filed into the auditorium, he handed those remaining to complete strangers.

Thankfully, given the amount spent by my extended family on programmes, the first night went well and even the critics seemed to enjoy it. There weren't many laughs in *The Country Girl*, which can err on the side of melo-drama at times, but when they did happen I could hear the comforting chortles of my dad that night in Greenwich.

It was an amazing experience and I met incredible people during the run, every night there was someone more interesting than the evening before, and it became impossible to drag myself away from the bar at the end of the evening. I don't know what I expected but I didn't recognise Vanessa Redgrave at all when she came to see her brother in the show. She was in the middle of filming *Mission Impossible* at the time and had her hair in a black pixie crop. She was very slim and dressed in a contemporary style so from the back I assumed her to be someone far younger. However, as soon as I saw those bright turquoise eyes, apparently free from make-up, I knew her face immediately. I felt terribly shy, even when she was kind about my performance after Corin introduced us. I was starstruck, hardly able to string a sentence together.

My dad, on the other hand, had no such problems. On the odd occasion he showed up at the theatre, he couldn't wait to get Corin and Kika talking about the latest socialist scandal. He loved all the backstage chat, he'd spent a lot of his formative years around theatre folk when Judith was an actress, and unlike me he never felt intimidated by anyone.

I continued to live at home in Kingston during the Greenwich run, as James, who had graduated drama school and won a role almost immediately, decamped to Worthing. Home was rather unsettled. Having been fired by the Mirror Group following the sudden death of Robert Maxwell in 1991, Dad was now editing for the 'other side', Rupert Murdoch's *Today* newspaper, a role for which he picked up the *What the Papers Say* award for Best Editor. Many of his *Mirror* staff had jumped ship and followed him to *Today* and they had gradually transformed the paper into a really decent left-leaning read for those young people now old enough to vote, and who, like me, had never known anything other than a Conservative government.

Being on his fifth Fleet Street editorship, my dad was no stranger to the threat of being sued. In 1990 Michael Jackson had tried to sue the *Mirror* for libel. They had printed a close-up photograph of Jackson which showed alarming cracks in his face. The accompanying article dared to suggest the cracks were the unfortunate result of too much cosmetic surgery. Jackson claimed the picture had been doctored, which of course it hadn't. When the case looked like it would run and run the judge demanded Jackson be examined by a doctor and amazingly Jackson agreed. My dad wrote in his 2002 autobiography *Dogs and Lampposts*:

'Unfortunately, the strange vagaries of our legal system prevent me from telling you any more about the visit or the trip around Jackson's face; both are covered by a confidentiality agreement. I can't tell you what the examination revealed, but I can say that, as a result of it, Britain was prevented from witnessing one of the finest libel spectacles for many a year.'

Five years later, a few weeks into the run of *The Country Girl*, I was standing alone in the dark of the wings at the side of the stage, awaiting my cue to enter, in tears, terrified that by the time I came off my dad would have been carted off to prison. Sometimes it's a challenge to squeeze out real tears on demand, other times they just come.

Dad had decided to publish part of a very revealing book about Prince Charles and Princess Diana written by their former housekeeper at Highgrove, Wendy Berry. *The Housekeeper's Diary: Charles and Diana Before the Breakup.* The book had been published worldwide and extracts were printed all over Europe, but somehow Prince Charles managed to get it banned in Britain on the grounds of confidentiality. Dad was outraged and went to press on the grounds that if Peter Wright could get away with publishing *Spycatcher* on account of it being available to the rest of the world, then they should be able to publish excerpts from the Wendy Berry book. He was wrong.

I came offstage at the end of the play that night to discover that, in the end, Dad got away with a reprimand from the judge who told him he was lucky to escape prison and fined him £25,000. Luckily *Today* footed the bill and Dad came home adamant that he would make the same decision again.

The Country Girl meant inevitably that the job at Episode had to end. Clare continued to work for the company as she was able to juggle it with small television parts. She was eventually relocated to Selfridges after a stint at the Brent Cross branch sapped her of the will to live. The area manager went on to recommend her for a managerial role within Episode. It often happens that what is intended as a temporary 'filler' job to pay the rent turns into something more permanent, and when the money is decent and regular it is easy to lose sight of your dream, especially when that dream can seem so far out of reach. However, Clare's passion for clothes didn't extend beyond buying them at discount for her own wardrobe, so scaling the heights of fashion retail wasn't to be. She stacked up a good selection of classy merchandise that far outweighed mine during her time on the shop floor, and then she moved on.

I found myself another part-time job, this time in a local hairdresser's near my mum and dad's in Kingston. James, with whom I had managed to buy a small flat in Battersea, was living in Paris while he toured with a theatre company based there.

With James away I kept myself busy writing off for acting jobs and writing articles I attempted to get published in magazines. I had imagined I would have no problem finding acting work after my successful debut in *The Country Girl* and I couldn't have been more wrong. My agent dutifully sent me off to loads of high-brow auditions but I didn't get any of them, I didn't have the confidence in my ability or my appearance to impress those casting Royal Shakespeare Company seasons or Merchant Ivory films.

So I started to write, and along the way I entered the *Vogue* talent competition which targeted young unpublished writers and offered them £1,000 prize money and work experience at the *Vogue* office. I wasn't particularly bothered about the work experience but I thought it would be good exercise for my brain. I submitted the three articles they requested the day before the closing date and promptly forgot about it.

It was when my dad phoned me at work at the hairdresser's to say an envelope had arrived from *Vogue* that I remembered the competition. I asked him to open the letter and then heard a huge cheer at the other end before Dad announced that I had been selected as one of the final ten and was invited to lunch at *Vogue* with the editor Alexandra Schulman and the competition judges, who included, among others, Nigella Lawson and fashion editor Lisa Armstrong. I was horrified and immediately went into a spin about what on earth I would wear for such an occasion. All of a sudden, nothing else mattered. I hadn't ever harboured any ideas of working for *Vogue*, but that didn't mean I didn't want to create an impression – the right impression preferably.

Meanwhile, I was doing quite a good job of finding my own not-quite-so-high-calibre roles through *PCR*. Call it aiming low, call it being more realistic about my chances, either way I was making progress and being offered small, low-paid jobs, which had to be better than failing to get any of the high-profile jobs my agent sent me up for.

One of the jobs I saw advertised in *PCR* involved five days filming in the Caribbean for Thomson Holidays, for which I would be paid £500. Not too shabby as jobs go.

The director Kerry Richardson was looking for two young actors to play a couple getting married on the beach in the Dominican Republic. The piece was to be filmed like a fly-on-the-wall documentary, meaning that there wouldn't be a script as such; we would rely on improvisation based around what the client, in this case Thomson Holidays, wanted.

On the day of the casting I arrived in a rather bad mood. I found out the day before that I had lost out on a role acting alongside the American actress and star of *Romancing the Stone* Kathleen Turner at Chichester Festival Theatre. Anyway, my 'laid-back' approach somehow worked for me and I was called back for a second audition. I was lucky Kerry and I hit it off immediately, and our shared sense of humour probably went a long way to securing me the part.

In the end I was very pleased to have such a plum job filming in the Caribbean but I was wary because I hadn't even met the actor, named Dan, who was to play my husband. Kerry assured me he was 'tall, dark and handsome', as if what the actor looked like was somehow the issue, but it had the effect of making me dread it even more.

Wardrobe and costume fittings come in all shapes and sizes in the acting world and are more often than not a very undignified affair. Kerry and her producer Stephanie Peat had already picked out the wedding gown they were borrowing for the shoot and so it quickly became clear the actress they chose would need to fit into this dress. Roles are won and lost for all sorts of reasons but this was the first time I was cast to fit into a dress. It was just as well that I hadn't lied on my CV about my measurements or there would have been a panic at the first wardrobe call.

After trying on the rather unsupportive, backless wedding dress, it became clear I wasn't going to be able to get away with going braless. Kerry lived near me in Clapham and we had discovered we shared a love of the hilariously old-fashioned Arding and Hobbs department store in Clapham Junction. Housed in a listed building opposite the station, now run by House of Fraser, it was the closest you could get to the Grace Brothers department store portrayed in the *Are You Being Served?* television series without having John Inman working in menswear. The kitsch nature of the place appealed to Kerry and me, and we decided that's where we'd meet.

The wedding dress, which had been tried on and chosen by Kerry herself, was a strappy-topped, big-skirted affair, meaning any bra worn would need to be backless, strapless and, for me, underwired. Being slim with big boobs always presents sartorial problems and I was dreading this trip to the lingerie department. Obviously we couldn't take the dress shopping with us so before leaving Kerry's house where we had discussed beachwear for the shoot – everything had to be a primary colour and classic in style, so the film would have longevity – Kerry drew the outline of the dress straps in felt-tip pen onto the top half of my body. If I hadn't found the process of trying on hundreds of bras and corsets while my chest was scrutinised by Kerry and the sales assistant so embarassing, I'd have thought it hilarious.

In the end we found a cream boned underwired corset with removable straps that did the trick. It was unbelievably hot to wear underneath a huge meringue wedding dress in the heat of the midday Caribbean sun, but it held my boobs up all day so I didn't care. If I genuinely had been getting married, as the various holidaymakers who stood up and clapped us on that Dominican Republic beach thought, my 'husband' wouldn't have found my sweat-drenched corset very attractive. However, at the end of the day's filming, our clothes (poor Dan was even worse off in a shirt and three-piece suit) were taken off to be dried out ready for the following day – such is the glamour of show business.

I had ended up meeting actor Dan for the first time before checking in at Gatwick airport. Unable to find Kerry or any of the crew at the designated area, we wandered off to get a coffee. It was a good way to break the ice at 5 a.m. on that crisp summer morning, but unfortunately our nattering meant we missed our names being called out ever more urgently over the tannoy. Unbeknown to us, Kerry was becoming more and more terrified that we'd both failed to turn up and was on her mobile phone trying to find two new actors when Dan and I strolled up, wondering what all the fuss was about. Still, it meant that by the time we filmed scenes as a loved-up, engaged couple drinking champagne in the plane, we had warmed up to each other a bit.

Despite Kerry's determination that we looked like the perfect couple, Dan and I didn't have much in common. He was a few years older than me and had graduated from Arts Educational around the same time as Clare's friend Hugo Speer, whom he knew. The acting profession is a small world, and you have to tread very carefully, because everyone knows everyone through someone else. Having been in the profession only a handful of years, I was only just starting out. I was on my best behaviour and having a whale of a time, whereas I suspect that for Dan it was just another job, albeit one with a lot of cocktails thrown in.

One afternoon, when the crew were filming some scenic shots for which Dan and I weren't needed, I took the opportunity to catch some rays while Dan borrowed a bicycle to explore the resort. Make-up artist Frankie was worried about letting us out of her sight in case we got sunburnt, which would have had serious implications for the continuity of the shoot. However, Dan and I begged her and she agreed on the condition that she herself applied a thick layer of sunscreen to both of us. We stood there like small children while she liberally slapped on the cream, Dan in his vest top and me in my bikini.

'Now off you go,' Frankie said. 'But whatever you do, reapply if you go in the sea.'

I had no intention of going anywhere: I had a sun

lounger and a book and some time off. I was in my element, and being paid for it!

A few hours later, I heard cries of horror coming from the set. Frankie was standing in front of a topless Dan, her head in her hands. Forgetting Frankie's warning, Dan had become hot while out cycling and removed his top. The result was a vest-shaped tan on Dan's torso where no sunscreen had been applied. But the wonders of fake tan and Frankie's expertise meant that problem was fairly easily solved. Two days later, when Dan accidentally shaved off one of his sideburns during a lunch break, Frankie had to draw it back in with an eyeliner so Kerry didn't notice when filming resumed. As I have mentioned, I am a hopeless giggler and I spent most of that afternoon trying not to laugh. When eventually the fake sideburn was revealed, I was ready to burst.

The shoot was fun, and it took my mind off an embarrassing incident that had happened a week before when I had my lunch at *Vogue*. I had decided, in my wisdom, to buy myself a white seventies-style trouser suit. If John Travolta in *Saturday Night Fever* springs to mind, then you're not far off track. The thing was, I wasn't really a *Vogue* reader, I tended to pick up *Elle* instead. Somehow, *Vogue* seemed more serious, more grown up and I didn't think of myself as all that grown up, despite being twenty-five years old.

Consequently, I assumed that all the people who worked at *Vogue* would be dripping in looks hot off the catwalk, perfectly accessorised, not a hair out of place. Silly really, I had grown up around journalists, admittedly the newspaper kind, but some of these people went on to women's magazines, indeed Lorraine Candy who worked for my dad went on to become editor of *Elle*.

Not that anybody tried to tell me better, but if they had I probably wouldn't have listened. I was going in a white trouser suit and that was that. The closest I could find to this Gucci catwalk look was a highly flammable one-button jacket and matching boot-cut trousers from the Vestry on the King's Road. I wore a black vest underneath and black platform sandals from Ravel. I felt fairly pleased with my outfit when I left the house but as I walked down the hill towards Clapham Junction station I started to feel vaguely self-conscious. By the time I got off the tube at Oxford Circus and approached Hanover Square it was raining and my white nylon suit was covered in tiny grey-coloured blobs. I did a circuit of Hanover Square before I had the courage to go in. This didn't help the suit but I was seriously considering giving the lunch a miss, so racked with terror was I. When I finally walked into the foyer, I felt all eyes on me. Most of the other nine finalists were already there and a quick scan of those gathered confirmed that yes, all nine of them (except the one male in the group) were dressed as if they might be going to a book club meeting somewhere in the Cotswolds.

I don't know how I got it so wrong. I sat there squirming in the uncomfortable damp nylon, head bowed, looking up from under my thrice-mascaraed lashes at all the pretty young ladies in twin sets and ladylike skirts and felt quite sick. I'd misjudged the dress code so horribly, I felt as if I was in one of those nightmares where you turn up at school assembly starkers, or at your own wedding with no make-up on. You know that episode of *Sex and the City* where Carrie gets drunk at (American) *Vogue*? It's embarrassing, yes, but at least she looks fabulous in her pinstripe Vivienne Westwood skirt suit, and she has a new 'do', and she is after all Carrie Bradshaw. I was sober, but kitted out like Tony Manero, without the swagger or the pout.

For the record, in 1997 the staff at *Vogue* dressed in cashmere cardigans, silk blouses, pearls and dainty heels with bare legs. Not one of them looked remotely like John Travolta, or even as if they had come straight off the Gucci runway.

I decided to enjoy my free lunch in the boardroom at *Vogue* and chatted to the judges cheerfully, because I felt all was lost anyway so I might as well have fun. Having the Caribbean job up my sleeve, I wasn't desperate to impress because I didn't ever think I was likely to win. One look at the tempting morsels laid out on the boardroom table put me into a panic about spillages and my head-to-toe white look, so I ate slowly and carefully and tried not to speak with my mouth full. In between courses, the judges moved places so they would have the chance to speak to all the finalists. I started off sitting next to Lisa Armstrong and then for the main course

I was served Nigella Lawson. I felt her looking at me as I carefully tucked into my food and when I next looked up she was smiling and asked me, 'So, Emily, what does your dad think of you getting this far in the *Vogue* competition?' My heart sank, she knew my dad. I mentally wrote myself out of the running. I had no idea Nigella Lawson knew my dad but, with the mention of his name, I had to assume he was the reason I'd won my place at the *Vogue* lunch and I felt deflated.

'He was really pleased,' I told Nigella, but try as I might, I couldn't think of anything else to say, no wise-crack, nothing. I was done. It was a shame but really didn't it matter more what *I* thought of being asked to come to lunch at *Vogue*? Perhaps it didn't.

Needless to say I was quite thankful when it was all over and I was able to go home, take off my white suit and relegate it to the dressing-up box.

◦◦◦

TIPS FOR SUCCESSFUL DRESSING

1. Let's start at the top, at the head, the inside of the head specifically. This is most important: only shop when you feel on top of your game. Try to avoid shopping with PMT or if you're feeling anything other than happy and positive. Many of us resort to retail therapy after a row or a bad day at work but rarely

will items purchased in this frame of mind prove to be suitable. As Dr Jennifer Baumgartner, the founder of a wardrobe-consulting business and a clinical psychologist, explains in her book *You Are What You Wear,* 'Our clothing is a reflection of what we are thinking and what we are feeling. Often, wardrobe mishaps are simply our inner conflicts bubbling to the surface.' Nobody wants their outfit reflecting a mind skewed by PMT, an outfit that says 'I'm failing, everyone thinks I'm crap, I'm so useless, everything's just so fucking awful all the time' – can you even imagine? I think I've made my point.

2. Style is knowledge. Knowing what works for your shape, your lifestyle and above all what you feel comfortable in, is paramount. This is where the French are so accomplished. Frenchwomen dress for themselves and don't pay much attention to trends or fads. I recently heard Caroline de Maigret, the French model and co-author of the hilarious *How to be Parisian Wherever You Are*, say she never feels jealous of a woman in a dress. Caroline simply doesn't do dresses; she prefers trousers, even on the red carpet. I would always feel jealous of a woman (or indeed a man) in a beautiful dress but that's me. Caroline's style – relaxed, boyish and effortlessly sexy – is quintessentially French because she is completely comfortable in herself. I know it's easier said than done (not to mention slightly nauseating) to say the secret is to learn to love the body you've been given

but oh, wouldn't it make getting dressed in the morning that much easier?

3. Never underestimate the importance of good under-wear, it can change your life. It's horses for courses, different outfits will require different underwear. Uplifting, smooth, barely there or horribly upholstered. Comfort is of the utmost importance, there's nothing more distracting and gruelling than knickers that are too tight or a bra that rubs. If you find a bra that works (and this inevitably will take a few wears to establish) then buy it in as many colours as you can afford. Also, bras should be renewed far more often than you think. Boobs change shape and size with age, pregnancy, child-birth and just where you happen to be in the month, for goodness' sake. Have a bra for every occasion and don't feel bad about it either: boobs can be a blessing for all sorts of reasons but they can literally drag you down. Show them who's boss.

4. Wearing the right colours for your skin tone and colour-ing will do wonders for your face. There are so many options other than black, which for the majority of people is the most unflattering shade to choose.

5. Likewise, being realistic about your shape and discovering what styles work for that shape is key. It's not as simple as skinny minnies like Kate Moss being able to wear anything, some clothes genuinely do require a bit more flesh to work really well. If you have a decent bust, necklines that throttle you simply won't be very

flattering. On the other hand, a scoop neckline on a flat chest will emphasise the boniness and lack of cleavage, so experiment with more interesting necklines; smaller chests can rock a poloneck or a boat neck for example. Generally speaking, you should avoid fuss (ruffles, bows, frills) if you're curvaceous but if you are looking to create curves these things can help create the illusion. You win some; you lose some: play to your strengths and focus on those areas you genuinely don't mind. Everyone has something about their bodies they like, even if it is their eyes or their ankles. I always make this the first thing I establish when I work with a client, no matter how intent they are on focusing on their 'bad points'.

6. Shoes are fabulous; they finish off an outfit, shopping for them is never dependent on whether or not you feel thin that day and they make you taller – how many other items in your wardrobe can claim that? I've lost count of the number of times I've seen a lovely, well thought out wedding outfit accessorised with a pair of bog standard black shoes presumably because 'well, black goes with everything'. Black shoes don't go with everything and get way too much airtime as it is, without being worn with summer dresses. Think outside the shoe box and experiment with sparkle, patterns and eye-popping colour – shoes can genuinely make an outfit.

7. Accessorising is in art and I'm not going to pretend it's an easy skill. But it is worth considering that a new bag, statement necklace or a fabulous hat can transform

an ordinary outfit into something really quite special. Approach with caution because you don't want to look – as my mum would say – like a Christmas tree, but don't shy away from accessories either. You've heard that Coco Chanel quote about removing one item before you leave the house, right? She knew some stuff, that Coco, so it's probably a tip worth bearing in mind. Personally, I wouldn't do big earrings and a big necklace simultaneously but I don't give a toss about shoes and bags matching. I'm all for mixing it up – a worn-in denim jacket over an evening dress, an evening dress with scruffy boots, boots with cut-off shorts, shorts with a designer tuxedo jacket. The choices are endless. I'm salivating just thinking about it.

8. I don't believe in buying things only when you need them. Items like jeans, bikinis and evening dresses, which can be strangely elusive when you are really desperate, should be bought when you find one that makes you feel a million dollars. Some of my most treasured pieces are those bought on a whim. But then I shop a lot and I enjoy it, I am rarely in the position of 'needing' something. Shopping because you have a genuine need for something immediately puts you under pressure and takes the fun out of it. As my shopping partner in crime Clare says, 'It stopped being about needing stuff a long time ago.'

৩৩

One day my agent called to tell me the well-respected casting director Michelle Guish who had cast *Four Weddings and a Funeral* and would go on to cast *Bridget Jones' Diary*, and whom I had met a couple of times, wanted me to meet with the television producer Beryl Vertue. Beryl was responsible for the *Men Behaving Badly* series and now had a new project in the offing, a comedy drama in a similar vein to the hugely successful *Cold Feet*. They wanted to see me for a walk-on part with one line, a waitress in a restaurant or something. This was all very exciting news. My agent went on to say she had arranged an appointment for me. The trouble was that it was right in the middle of a day's shooting for a pop video for an unknown singer by the name of CB Milton who was very big in Belgium, apparently. I was scheduled to film for the day at Cafe de Paris just off Leicester Square.

The day was an unusually hot one in August and as the appointment was at Teddington Studios I was hopelessly in the wrong place at the wrong time. I had accepted the pop video gig on the sly so I wouldn't have to part with the obligatory 12 per cent fee, so there was no asking my agent to sort it out for me. Instead, I forfeited lunch, made my excuses to the video director and hot-footed it to Waterloo station where I caught a train to Teddington, a good thirty-five minutes away. By the time I had legged it from Teddington station to the studios in the unforgiving midday sun, I was not looking my best. Out of breath and feeling very sweaty, I changed my trainers for a pair of smart shoes so I looked vaguely like I might work in an office, reapplied my lipstick and hoped for the best. It wasn't until I got into the lift to see the director and producer waiting for me upstairs, that I had the chance to check out my reflection in the mirror. It had completely slipped my mind that earlier that day I had been styled for a pop video. My bobbed hair had been backcombed to within an inch of its life and hairsprayed outwards so I resembled some sort of sun god. My make-up was dark purple and heavy and there was glitter. And all this on top of a conservative trouser suit. Nobody on the train had batted an eyelid at my appearance, this is Great Britain after all, and I was in such a panic about the audition that I had my head buried in the script for the whole journey.

It was far too late to do anything about my bizarre appearance once in that lift so I took a deep breath and used it to my advantage. It wasn't every day I was able to claim I was fitting in a casting in my lunch break. I felt instantly more employable than I ever had done before in the same situation. I read from the script and chatted confidently with those present. I knew it had gone well when I got back in the lift but also I was very relieved it was over and I hadn't been late. I got back on the train to Waterloo and finished the day's filming.

A couple of days later my agent called.

'Well, they really liked you . . .' this was her usual opening gambit, I waited for the 'but' . . .

'But I'm afraid they didn't think you were quite right for the part in the restaurant.'

'Oh well, never mind, thanks anyway—'

'They want you for a bigger part, a character with three episodes – congratulations!'

You can't beat one of those telephone calls. If only they came more often.

Feeling more flush than I had in some time, I allowed myself a trip to Selfridges in Oxford Street where the wealth of brands was unrivalled. A decade before when model Nick Kamen had stripped off his Levi's in the launderette, there had been only one brand to be seen in, but by now the craze for Levi 501s had passed and where oversized jeans pulled in with a belt had been the thing in the late eighties, now the silhouette was altogether more streamlined. Italian denim brands such as Replay and Diesel were emerging as the latest names in denim with a variety of washes, cuts and rises. Designers who had previously given denim a wide berth were now producing far sleeker styles with the high-end price tag to match.

Frederik Willems joined Levi's in 1999 and was one of the designers of the engineered or 'twisted' jean. 'Levi's created the engineered jean because young people stopped buying 501s,' explains Fred. 'The three-dimensional shape of the jeans was influenced by the ergonomic trend that was appearing in lots of products – the Apple Mac computer and the re-modelled Beatle car, for example.'

The Selfridges denim department now boasted a 'Bodymetrics' measuring machine which ascertained which styles will fit you perfectly. I invested in a pair of Earl Jeans – the word on the street was that they lengthened the leg – and slowly the penny dropped that just as a well-cut jacket could slim the waist, so a long and lean pair of jeans with strategically placed back pockets could make your legs look longer and your bottom more pert.

When I didn't have an acting role to occupy me, I had time to drum up more work or write. It was while flicking through the back pages of the industry newspaper *The Stage* that I came across an advert: 'Mystery Shoppers Wanted'.

I knew about mystery shopping from the time at Episode when Clare and I had a brush with one. There were few skills and requirements listed in the advert beyond attention to detail and an ability to write good English. It seemed too good to be true, so I applied for a job with this company based in the north of England and then started to sniff around to see if there were further similar opportunities up for grabs.

My application for the mystery-shopping company advertised in *The Stage* took the form of an assignment to a mobile phone shop of my choice in the area where I lived. I was to visit the outlet and then write up my experience by hand and send it back to the company to evaluate the report.

At this time, the late 1990s, the mobile phone industry had taken off and there was an abundance of retail outlets on the high street, all trying to outdo one another with amazing deals, ever-smaller handsets and ultimately – and this was where the mystery shopping came in – a fabulous personalised customer service experience. Within walking distance of my flat in Clapham Junction there were at least six different mobile phone shops. All those brands vying for business and most of them employing mystery-shopping companies not just to test their own staff but also to spy on the competition. In the early days of mystery shopping, it would not be unusual for me to report on three mobile phone shops in the same street, all giving me reasons why they were better than their competitors. It was hardcore face-to-face selling and unbelievably competitive.

My report did the trick and I was signed up with the mystery-shopping company. I clocked up a few hours a week, going to different branches of high-street chains, from pet stores to Italian restaurants, shoe repairers to lingerie boutiques.

Obviously, my training as an actor meant that pretending to be a genuine customer wasn't a problem for me. Coupled with the writing that I had always done as a hobby, and my memory for the most random of details, mystery shopping and I were a perfect fit – and I discovered I quite enjoyed it too. Each visit usually took no longer than fifteen minutes, if that, and I enjoyed shopping of any kind so it felt quite natural to me. I could pick and choose when I worked and the areas I visited.

I didn't leave anything to chance and would read and then re-read the instructions and the questionnaire to ensure I didn't miss anything that needed to be observed or asked. Back then it genuinely did feel rather, well, mysterious. You tended to forget that to other customers, and hopefully to the majority of the staff, you are just another customer needing help in a day filled with customers who need help. Sometimes, I wondered how on earth I was getting away with it . . .

'Can you please tell me what equipment I would need to set up a fish tank at home?'

(Hmm, they look suspicious . . . Do I really look like someone who wants fish in their house? Am I too young to look like I need a fish tank? Or am I too old?)

'I want to buy my brother a pay as you go phone but I'm not sure how I go about it . . .'

(What if they ask how much call time he needs? Oh shit, what was the budget I was supposed to give?)

It was a relief once the scenario was complete and I was able to make my excuses and leave, but that was the easy bit. Sitting down after the event to write it all up was more time-consuming, though once done I didn't give it another thought.

It remained a huge novelty to those around me, however, and on the occasions where I needed a partner in crime, for example when I started to report on restaurants, that was when things started to get a bit more complicated.

Each month I was allocated lunch or dinner with a well-known chain and, although I could dine alone, more often than not I would take a friend or family member along with me. As an actress often strapped for cash I loved being able to buy people a nice meal. I became fairly sick of eating from the same menu but a lot of people benefitted from this particular assignment and I soon came to know who could be trusted to be undercover versus those who were slightly less comfortable with the covert nature of the task. In this sort of restaurant scenario where there is a budget and many guidelines to stick to, you really need to brief your dining companion fully before you sit down at your table. I didn't always do this, and it would be to my cost.

My friend Rich, a financial advisor and always one with an eye on expenditure, would ask in front of the waiter or waitress, 'Am I allowed to have a beer?' which made me look some sort of control freak. My mum, on the other hand, would freeze and not say anything at all. Finally, there are those who revel in the novelty of the whole experience and fancy themselves a bit of an actor, throwing themselves into the prescribed role with gusto. My dad fell into this category and during my first ever restaurant visit – a branch in Kingston-upon-Thames – insisted on accepting every offer of starters, side dishes, extra drinks, puddings and coffees, thereby completely blowing the fairly meagre budget. When I objected, Dad waved me off saying he would pay the bill so it wasn't a problem. This of course was a problem as it was supposed to be me filing the expenses. As it turned out, my dad wouldn't let me pay him back for the bill either and so I ended up getting paid for a meal I hadn't forked out a thing for. That was my dad all over.

My mum had good reason to act like a rabbit caught in the headlights during mystery-shopping meals. I was carrying out a fairly run-of-the mill visit to the Woking branch of a small regional lingerie shop. I had done several of these visits before and was familiar with the brief, which involved being measured for a bra and trying some styles on while monitoring how many questions the staff member asked me, how many styles they suggested and how many additional items, such as knickers and suspender belts, I was offered.

My mum offered to drive me so, as she parked up, I jumped out of the car and went to start my enquiry. I was in the middle of a conversation about underwear sets when my mum came in and proceeded to browse the rails, making a concerted effort not to catch my eye. I didn't think anything of it until a little later when I was trying things on in the fitting room at the back of the shop, I heard one of the shop staff asking the assistant who was serving me, 'Did you see what happened to the blond woman in the navy jacket who was in here?' She sounded panicky. I knew the customer to whom she referred could be none other than my mum. 'I think she may have left without paying for something . . .'

I went cold. I knew my mum hadn't stolen anything and could only think she looked suspicious because she was trying to avoid meeting my eye. I had no choice other than to continue with my brief and as I hurriedly got dressed and made my way to the counter to pay for my purchases as instructed, the second assistant sped out of the shop in pursuit of my mum, who was oblivious to the drama unfolding in her wake.

A few minutes later the shop assistant came steaming back into the shop out of breath and with my mum in tow. My mum was also out of breath and very red-faced. The shop assistant appeared to be holding a red satin negligee with red fur trim, an item she had not had with her when she had previously left the shop.

'I'm *so* sorry . . .' my mum blurted out, 'I really had no idea, it must have just attached itself to me while I was looking at something else, I can assure you it wasn't intentional!'

I kept my head down and studied the credit-card machine with unnatural concentration as my mum continued to protest her innocence. It went on . . .

'I mean, really this isn't the sort of thing someone my age would buy, is it? You must be able to see this isn't my sort of thing?'

Eventually Mum was allowed to leave the shop and I followed soon after. I found my mum sitting in her car looking like a naughty child. Naturally, she was very apologetic. What I was most concerned about was whether I should write this incident up in my report. Under normal circumstances I wouldn't have thought twice as anything that affects your shopping experience needs to be documented, but this was my mum. I decided to write the incident up and play it down, giving the staff credit for fetching 'the customer' back in time.

It made a great family dinner table story, the tale of Mum and the slutty underwear she stole in Woking. My dad laughed so much, he actually clutched his sides. Needless to say, Mum never tried to muscle in on any of my assignments again. And when she was invited to come along she would keep very quiet for the duration so she couldn't be accused of putting her foot in it again.

CHAPTER FIVE

The Pink Wellington Boots

I n the end, the 1990s would not be defined by the recession early in the decade. Although the ailing economy inevitably meant less disposable income to spend on high-end fashion, for chains such as New Look and Primark, the recessionary climate saw a growth spurt. It was no coincidence when the grunge look took off, its dishevelled, laid-back aesthetic the perfect antidote to the conspicuous consumption of the previous decade. Grunge encouraged unstructured layering of second-hand or home-made clothes, messy unwashed hair and slept in make-up, as demonstrated by the likes of Kurt Cobain and Courtney Love. This was a street style, however, and it didn't go down well with high-end consumers who didn't want to pay designer prices for such a negligent look which, in any case, didn't suit their lifestyle. Marc Jacobs, who in 1992 was designing at Perry Ellis, sent the models in his 'grunge' collection catwalk show – a homage to the Seattle music scene – out in floral print button-up dresses, cashmere thermals and Doc Marten boots. He was fired soon afterwards. Grunge was over, relegated back to the charity shops from whence it came.

However, the desire for so-called street style was still there. Tommy Hilfiger with its preppy branding was adopted by those into hip-hop, and old-school Puma and Adidas trainers became incredibly popular. Sean Farrell remembers this time well at Office London. 'We were bang on with club and street fashion at the time. We designed a whole range of disco dolly sandals in about ten colours and they got loads of press, we sold thousands. [It was the same with] Caterpillar boots, we went a whole year without having to go into sale, we just didn't need to.' Sean admits it sounds surprising but explains that the recession didn't affect the Office customer. 'Many of our customers still lived at home with their parents and in a recession the kids don't feel it as much. They were all out raving and so were we.' Certainly, when I first met Sean, later on in the 1990s, he always seemed to be having a great time and was doing well, a low point being when his Oswald Boateng suit disappeared from the carousel at Las Vegas airport en route to his wedding.

The high-end fashion world meanwhile was witnessing

the emergence of supermodels, a group of five women marketed by their agencies as not merely clothes horses but personalities too. After Linda Evangelista, Claudia Schiffer, Christy Turlington, Cindy Crawford and Naomi Campbell appeared together on the cover of *Vogue* they were cast in the video for George Michael's single 'Freedom', which became the tip of a very lucrative iceberg. They commanded enormous fees – prompting the infamous Evangelista quote about not getting out of bed for less than $10,000 a day – and sparked a new trend for models as celebrities: opening their own restaurants, Barbie dolls being made in their image and fitness videos promising a supermodel body. Sure, there had been famous models before, Twiggy in the sixties and Lauren Hutton in the seventies to name just two, but this was different. Here was a group of women earning far more than any man in the same industry could ever hope for and simultaneously changing the face of fashion. Cindy Crawford, the epitome of the All-American Girl, was instrumental in bringing back the more curvaceous fashion silhouette, a look that lent itself perfectly to the sumptuous designs of a certain Italian designer, Gianni Versace.

After employing the services of 'the Supers' for his 1994 campaign, Versace attracted the interest of the world's most photographed woman, now not only a confident thirty-four-year-old but newly single. Princess Diana's style took on a new lease of life following the breakdown of her marriage to Prince Charles. She was regularly pictured leaving the gym in tiny shorts and posed for covers for *Vogue* and *Vanity Fair* wearing Versace. The princess and the designer became close friends.

That same year, a little-known actress, the girlfriend of Hugh Grant, star of the latest British film *Four Weddings and a Funeral*, made headlines when she borrowed a Versace gown to wear to the London premiere. Elizabeth Hurley became a household name overnight courtesy of a plunging black dress that held her curves in place with giant safety pins. She won an Estee Lauder cosmetics contract and a career that owed little to her acting talents. Celebrity culture was taking off and glamour and showiness was back in style and we all wanted a piece of it. Even if we couldn't afford it.

It had never been easier than it was in the 1990s to open multiple store cards. Department stores and retail chains had to up their game in order to remain relevant in the difficult economic climate, and so were constantly running incentives and promotions. I had credit cards but I kept a lid on them. I knew people who weren't so lucky and the pain of getting further and further into the red was becoming all too common as twenty-somethings juggled paying off student debts with a lifestyle that went hand in hand with living in London.

In 1994 the Sears group who owned Selfridges launched a £94-million redevelopment programme, which included the introduction of their iconic yellow bag. The plans to modernise and declutter the store were initially mocked but ultimately the changes drew in a younger, more fashionable customer, and where Selfridges led, M&S, Debenhams and House of Fraser attempted to follow. Other less adaptable department stores fell by the wayside.

Shopping for everything under one roof continued to be an attractive prospect, especially when that roof was home to such a wide variety of products, from designer labels to the more affordable high-street fashion accessible to all.

Once more between acting jobs, I took a part-time job as a receptionist at Thomas Pink, whose head office was based not far from where we lived in Battersea. It was my dad who first introduced me to this very British brand. He liked the roomy shirts they produced and often shopped at the small Chancery Lane branch close to his New Fetter Lane offices. In 1998, Thomas Pink had just started to produce women's shirts and the company was expanding. It was a good time to become part of it, the financial worries that had plagued the country in the beginning of the decade now largely a memory.

Almost as soon as I was offered the job at Thomas Pink, I landed the role in *Wonderful You*. It was embarrassing having to ask for time off almost in my second week there and they must have wondered what they had let themselves in for. Luckily, my boss Sophy was understanding, and from then on it worked very well; I did extra shifts when required and they gave me time off for acting jobs when I needed it. What started as a short-term job to pay the mortgage, soon materialised into a secure regular job.

James and Peter Mullen (along with a third brother John who lived in Portugal) were forty-something Irishmen who had reportedly started the company because they were fed up with their shirttails coming out of their trousers. Both measuring in at well over six foot tall, they worked on the top floor and kept themselves to themselves. I didn't have much to do with them but it was a relaxed atmosphere in the office and I enjoyed being in an environment where I was just as likely to be asked my opinion about a new fabric print as sort through the day's post.

It was at Thomas Pink one day that I met shop guru Mary Portas whose PR company Yellow Door represented Thomas Pink. Mary had worked her way up from visual merchandiser (window dresser) at Harrods to advising on the Harvey Nichols refurbishment at the start of the decade. I shared the reception area with her only briefly as she waited to meet with James Mullen, and yet her mere presence silenced me. She was clearly a force to be reckoned with and in the five or ten minutes she was there made no secret of her horror at our decidedly insalubrious office space.

Affordable fast fashion was becoming ever more available and the high street was getting better and better at reproducing covetable catwalk looks quicker than you could say 'designer rip-off'. The leader in this arena soon emerged as little-known Spanish retailer Zara.

First opened in Spain in 1975 by Armancio Ortega, Zara started off life called Zorba, in reference to the film *Zorba the Greek*. After a nearby bar owner pointed out his bar was already called Zorba, Ortega was forced to rethink. The cheapest solution, since the shop front was already made up, was to find a name that used most of the same letters. Zara was born.

In 1989 Ortega had opened branches in the USA, with London's Regent Street branch following in 1998. With half of the manufacturing done in Europe rather than Asia, Zara's twice-weekly deliveries of hot-off-the-catwalk imitations took the quality and quantity of the high-street offering to a new level.

This same year, Hennes & Mauritz (the name by which the Swedish brand had been known since 1968 following the acquisition of hunting apparel brand Mauritz Widforss) changed their name. For those born after 1990, 'H&M' was the fabulous new go-to glossy white store for affordable trends; for the rest of us, it would always be 'Hennes' – a sure-fire way of showing your age where Botox had blurred the lines.

Suddenly, where once upon a time Kingston-upon-Thames had been one of very few places to shop at Hennes, there were branches of H&M popping up all over the place. Shops opened to great fanfare in Paris and New York (I happened to visit both cities soon after the openings and witnessed the excitement with my own eyes), places where cheap and cheerful fashion had never been seen on this scale previously and further proof that the European high street was head and shoulders above the rest of the world.

Where Zara led, another Spanish brand by the name of Mango soon followed. Established in 1984 in Barcelona, like Zara, Mango's concept was based on the idea of bringing the brand 'closer to the largest number of women'. Unlike the traditional department store concept of different brands targeting different age groups, this new breed of fashion emporium was offering fashion for all ages, all lifestyles and almost every occasion, from teenager to grandparent, under the same roof with a price point everyone could afford. Zara, Mango and the new improved H&M breathed new life into womenswear retail and the comparable British brands hit the ground running.

As the nineties drew to a close, my equilibrium was jolted. I had settled down relatively early with my boyfriend James, we had a joint mortgage by the age of twenty-five, and although our acting jobs took us to different places and with different people, our six-year relationship was solid. Until one day it wasn't. We were the best of friends but almost without either of us noticing, James and I started to drift apart. I had wanderlust and the advent of cheap airlines and the freedom our rather unstructured lives offered made me want to travel as much as possible, but James wasn't so keen. In the end, it was a mutual decision to go our separate ways. It was sad, but not devastating, and although it would be at least a year before we properly divided up our finances, we remained very close throughout. There were no recriminations and this was largely down to the very lovely and patient man James is.

His magnanimous attitude even extended to genuine happiness for me when I very quickly met and started a relationship with financial advisor Richard. We met in a bar in Battersea, on the rare occasion that he wasn't wearing a suit.

Going out with someone with the same name as my dad was not only a first for me but something I found painfully embarrassing. In fact, it wasn't until a good six months after we first met that I even introduced him to my family and friends. I referred to him only as 'that bloke' so I didn't have to speak his name out loud. I managed to call him all sorts of names, so never found it necessary to use the name Richard. A therapist would have a field day with that one, I'm sure.

Rich Brace was from all over. He was born in Devon but moved around the country with his dad's job, meaning he was never in one school for very long. This turned him into the sort of adult who is not only brilliant when meeting new people and making small talk, but who is the ultimate problem solver. However, despite his ability to be at home in new situations, even Rich wasn't quite prepared for meeting my parents for the first time. He had resisted it for as long as possible, but when the dreaded day came he dutifully accompanied me to the family home in Kingston, where my mum, dad and siblings awaited with interest the arrival of this new boyfriend, a novelty after six years of James who had become part of the furniture.

I am more aware now I am older that many people were nervous about meeting my dad as his reputation tended to precede him. The stereotype caricature of a newspaper editor made him seem scary, I suspect. In reality, although my dad could certainly be brusque and mischievous, he couldn't have been further from the cigar-smoking, braces-wearing, world-weary hack so often portrayed in films about the newspaper world. He did keep our new boyfriends at arm's length initially and rarely thought any of those brought home good enough for my sister and me. What father does?

So when Rich and I walked into the kitchen in Kingston that Sunday lunchtime, my dad had scuttled off leaving my mum to welcome the stranger. Everyone loves my mum; she is warm, gorgeous and fun. She too was moved around a lot as a child, attending many different schools, so like Rich she is comfortable meeting new people and the two got on well. Then my dad appeared.

'Dad, this is Rich, Rich this is my dad, Richard . . .'

'Richard, hello, I'm Richard.'

Cue uncomfortable laughter, although not from my

dad, who is not uncomfortable in the slightest and has moved on to the far more important issue of getting drinks for everyone.

Rich was a handy man to have around, not least because of his aptitude for numbers and sensible financial advice. I am good with money generally, mostly because as an actor you often don't have any. Store cards charged an outrageous amount in interest and really had no benefit beyond whatever the tempting opening offer was. It was thanks to Rich that I cut up all those store cards and settled with just the one credit card I used for mystery-shopping purchases and for which I was later reimbursed – all the air miles and none of the expense!

The 'noughties', as the first decade of the twenty-first century became known, was a defining moment for the high street. There was a backlash against the brash branding and logos favoured in the late nineties, which was brought to a head by the popularity of new HBO series *Sex and the City*. The billboards that went up all over London in the weeks preceding the pilot episode caused a hype the like of which I had not seen before. The poster of the four actresses who played the four main characters were dressed in little black dresses of different styles, simple and yet strong and stylish. As a woman soon to be thirty myself, the timing couldn't have been better. I wasn't overly impressed by the first series but I stuck with it and by the second series I was addicted.

Most women loved it and were utterly drawn in to the fashion-led, dating obsessed lifestyle portrayed in the series. On-going debates ranged from whether you were a Carrie, a Miranda, a Charlotte or a Samantha, to whether you were 'pro-Big' or 'pro-Aidan'. I think the male population was a little bemused, if not horrified, by many of the storylines. This was girl power all grown up and wreaking havoc on New York City. The Spice Girls' dress sense may have divided opinion but Carrie Bradshaw took fashion to a whole different level. Here was an independent woman not only choosing a designer shoe collection over a mortgage, but the commitment-phobic bad-boy boyfriend over the decent diamond-giving home lover.

At its peak *Sex and the City* attracted 10.6 million viewers and under the eye of veteran costume designer Patricia Field, the unique styling of the clothes – a mix of vintage, designer and high-street pieces – was a talking point all of its own. Both Sarah Jessica Parker and her sex-columnist character Carrie Bradshaw became synonymous with an eye-catching style that widened the goal posts in terms of age-appropriate dressing. Individuality became key and nothing, not even a pink tutu, was out of bounds.

Rich and I split up after a year – although we remained good friends – which meant that I was single for more or less the first time in my adult working life, while most of my friends who had been single during their twenties were now properly coupled up for the onset of their thirties. My thirties would prove to be a merry-go-round of short-lived affairs, some ill-advised and painful, some good clean(ish) fun. In the neighbourhood where I lived in Battersea the social life was fun and vibrant with many bars and restaurants, ideal for girls' nights out and uncomfortable first dates from which you might need to make a quick exit.

One evening, my schoolfriend Sara and I were having dinner in a restaurant on the rather chi-chi Northcote Road in Battersea when she mentioned that her boyfriend Stew was in the vicinity with an old friend from school in tow. She suggested we all meet up and go for a drink later on. We both jumped with fright when suddenly there was a loud splat on the huge window next to us as the tanned, bare torso of a young man, face obscured by the T-shirt pulled over his head, was pressed against the window. Sara's boyfriend Stewart's grinning face appeared alongside the torso. The arms attached to the torso then peeled the T-shirt away to reveal, posing through the glass at us, Stew's mate Steve. But this wasn't just any Steve, this was *Just 17* model competition winner Steve, the one who got his haircut in Vidal Sassoon when I worked behind the reception desk. Fucking hell – *that* Steve! Small world.

I am in shock. I am not calm. I have so many questions to ask and I don't even know what they are. I just know I am not wearing the outfit I would have planned to be wearing had I known this was going to happen. Again.

The four of us met up as planned and I met Steve Wells properly. We didn't get on and it was incredibly disappointing. He needled me and I sniped back. Poor Steve, he couldn't possibly have lived up to the image of perfection I had imagined and nor would he want to. Having wrung as much out of the modelling industry as he could, Steve had moved into IT. The final straw had come when he was told by his model booker, a then unknown Davina McCall, that he would never hit the big time as a model on account of his overly large nostrils. I thought I'd zoned in on and developed a complex about every area of my body but even I had never worried about my nostrils. Go figure. How lucky for me then that Steve Wells had no preconceived ideas about me – he had no recollection of ever meeting me before and this was the stance he took on the next few occasions when our paths crossed. He would give me a peck on the cheek and say, 'Hi Emily, I don't think we've met . . .' I never knew whether this was his own particular brand of wind up or if I'd made so little impression that he genuinely had no idea who I was each time.

The self-employed writer who spent her days tapping away on her laptop in her local coffee shop and her nights drinking cocktails with her friends in Manhattan's coolest bars was a lifestyle which appealed enormously to me. My dad now had his own weekly political column in the *Sunday Mirror* and was also writing his autobiography so, with little idea of what I was doing, I started to daydream about feature writing myself; I wasn't very confident after the *Vogue* incident and knew that simply fancying myself as Carrie Bradshaw probably wasn't going to cut it should I ever find myself in close proximity of anyone from *Vogue* again.

My sister Hannah, now married, had worked in production at Sky News for several years when one day she called to say that Sky News Active was being revamped and they wanted someone to cover London Fashion Week with up-to-the-minute news stories from the shows. I was thrilled, but knew some serious time management was required. My boss Sophy at Thomas Pink was great whenever I had taken time off at the last minute to do an acting job but London Fashion Week would be five days of back-to-back catwalk shows in locations all over London, so I would have to devote myself to it completely for the duration. Fortunately I was able to take a week's holiday from the day job.

There was the added complication that I would need to file copy whenever possible – there was no Wi-Fi in 2003 – and the responsibility of getting to and from each show and what stories to focus on would be entirely down to me. Could I do it? It would be an enormous challenge and I didn't know if I was up to the job. The money Sky agreed to was way more than I was expecting and as a rookie I wondered if they knew the risk they were taking. My sister, far braver than me, issued me with a press pass and told me to stop being ridiculous, I would be fine. I was excited but nervous; what on earth would I wear each day?

Twenty-four-hour rolling news had been around for a while, but if Sky could get the pictures alongside hot-off-the-catwalk information, they would be way ahead of the following day's newspapers. You never knew what might happen at London Fashion Week – when Naomi Campbell fell off a pair of Vivienne Westwood platforms in 1994 it made front-page news. A mere thirty-second appearance on a catwalk by Kate Moss could catapult a designer to fame and a Designer at Debenhams contract overnight. London designers were known for taking risks and presenting far more quirky and experimental collections. I really had no idea what I was doing but I knew I would thoroughly enjoy spending the day watching fashion shows, something I had longed to do since I was a child, so I tried not to think too much about the logistics.

I was lucky, I learnt from the best. Dad was still an editor when newspaper production progressed from being mapped out on paper on a desk to being designed on a computer, but he was old-school Fleet Street and didn't need a laptop or the Internet to get a story done. In the summer of 2005 I took part in the London Triathlon and the news came through that the Labour Politician Robin Cook had died suddenly while out hiking. *Sunday Mirror* editor Tina Weaver had worked her way up under my dad's editorship and had achieved acclaim with her investigative work on Michael Jackson. On taking over the editorship of the *Sunday Mirror*, she asked Dad to write a weekly column. This particular Saturday afternoon, Tina was on the phone asking Dad to write Robin Cook's obituary for the following day's edition. Being in the middle of a noisy sporting event only made it more fun for my dad who jotted his thoughts down on a napkin in the pub where we were all celebrating the end of my race. He then dictated the obituary to the *Mirror* newsdesk over the telephone. Job done. As long as I got the words down after each catwalk show, the rest would take care of itself.

Luckily, fashion shows rarely run to schedule and, although I missed a few (once because they simply wouldn't let me in and once because I got on a bus going in the wrong direction), I saw 80 per cent of the shows and reported twice a day.

It was the second time I would come into contact with British designer Katharine Hamnett. Her autumn/winter show, which was held in a dark and damp basement venue somewhere off Ladbroke Road in west London, featured outsized slogan T-shirts screaming 'STOP THE WAR' and 'BLAIR OUT'. The collection reprised her earlier eighties T-shirts, the 'CHOOSE LIFE' slogan winning immense publicity when worn by Wham! in their 'Wake Me Up Before You Go-Go' video.

At the beautiful Pringle show held in Holland Park, I was lucky enough to find myself directed to the front row. The front row isn't as starry in London as in the other three cities, Paris, New York and Milan, but you might nab a goody bag, even if it isn't anything like the swag you tend to pick up in New York – no mobile phones or jewels. I did get my hands on a lovely Pringle cashmere hair band though.

Another show, I forget whose, was running spectacularly late even by fashion week standards. I was kept waiting outside in the cold for an age, despite having both a Sky News pass and an invitation. I was eventually let in by the burly security crew with moments to go before the lights went down. I was ushered in by one of the many pretty blond PR girls carrying a clipboard and directed to quickly take the empty seat on the front row. You can't have an empty space on the front row so I got lucky. I eyed the goody bag greedily but acted as if I was absolutely entitled to be there. With a confident flick of my hair and a quick glance to my left I realised I was sitting next to none other than *Vogue* editor Alexandra Schulman.

Should I say something? Would she remember me as the girl who turned up to lunch at *Vogue* as John Travolta? Should I make a joke about it? And when it came down to it, did I look any better today?

I caught Ms Schulman looking me up and down briefly and couldn't work out whether she was wondering what the hell I was wearing or simply who I was, quite possibly it was too dark for her to see anything much. It didn't make any difference, I sat there trying out various little chats with her in my head and then the music started and the lights came up. I didn't have the courage to say anything to her. I'm rubbish like that, no good at small talk.

So nobody was more surprised than me when at the Julien McDonald show I managed the scoop of my very short career. At the time Julien McDonald was enjoying a moment, and his amazing spider's web dresses and barely there catsuits were appearing on the back of all sorts of fabulous beings. His show was staged at the Roundhouse in Camden and it was scheduled for around 10 p.m. I was lucky to get in, the crowd was rowdy and many people didn't have invitations so the closer it got to show time, the more hysterical people became.

I managed to get in and find my seat, somewhere miles from the runway but with a decent bird's eye view of the collected audience.

And then I saw her, or rather her shiny tomato red hair, sitting in the front row patiently looking around. It was Patricia Field, costume designer for *Sex and the City*. Sarah Jessica Parker had recently given birth, meaning most of the previous series had been shot with Carrie Bradshaw either in voluminous dresses or carrying huge bags in front of her stomach so the bump was almost (but not always) covered up. After making a quick call to my dad for courage, I took a deep breath, elbowed my way through the overexcited crowds and introduced myself to the very friendly and charming Ms Field. She was more than happy to chat and we discussed dressing a pregnancy so that it didn't look like a pregnancy, creating a pregnancy in a dress where there wasn't one and then styling post-pregnancy. There was a lot of pregnancy both real and unreal in that particular series. I was up very late that night editing my articles and emailing them off to Sky, but I couldn't stop grinning about my exclusive interview.

I had never worked so hard. It was exhausting. Fair play to those fashion journalists who do all four fashion weeks twice a year, every year. The pace and the pressure to look good is relentless and, even if you have a limo and a comfortable hotel room to retreat to at the end of the night, your head is so full of fashion you start to crave your pyjamas and a box set of *ER*. But I loved it. My pieces went down well with Sky, who often managed to get my breaking fashion stories up on their site well before anyone else had a chance. I felt very proud and started to think perhaps I had actually done quite a good job. I made some fairly shaky statements in the heat of the moment and some of my predictions were a little off kilter, but I seemed to get away with it. Maybe that's what everyone's doing, I thought, perhaps everyone is winging it. Sky asked if I would be interested in covering the following season's shows too. Getting away with it didn't feel too bad at all.

On Monday morning it was back to work behind the reception desk at Thomas Pink. I picked up acting jobs whenever they popped up, and did a few bits and pieces for the *Sunday Mirror*, *London Lite* and *Take a Break* magazine. I also continued my scourge on the high street with regular mystery-shopping assignments, which was a useful way to keep the acting and writing strings in tune. Over time I was offered assignments to every business and service imaginable, from the Post Office to Bond Street jewellers, leisure centres to funeral parlours. All these establishments wanted feedback on things they are and, more importantly, are not doing right. Even with three years at drama school, sometimes the scenario you were required to follow could be skin-crawlingly out of one's comfort zone. I have discovered all too late after accepting work that my role is to enquire at a pharmacy about medication for constipation, to ask at a customer service desk if it is all right to return sheets that have been slept in or to visit a nursery with a view to sending my small (very small, in fact, non-existent) child there. None of these things sit easily with me.

But of course life is full of uncomfortable scenarios for which there is no precedent. An early visit to a shoe repair chain left me lost for words when I went in with a pair of shoes needing re-heeling. The brief was to ask to have them done straight away. The staff member on duty told me he wouldn't be able to do them immediately and so I asked how long I might have to wait for them to be ready. The staff member thought about it, you could almost hear the process, before replying with absolutely no sense of irony, 'Well, I gotta go toilet first . . .'

Not so funny was the time my younger sister Hannah and I went one evening for a meal at an Italian restaurant just off Leicester Square. Hannah had not long got married and had a new baby, Phoebe, so I didn't see as much of her as I'd have liked, and when the opportunity for dinner for two came up I invited her along.

We had the giggles from the moment we arrived, firstly because we were seated at a table in the corner right next to the door to the kitchen. This not only meant we were bumped into as waiters rushed in and out of the kitchen but also afforded us a perfect view into the not altogether professional goings on in the staff area. If you've ever worked behind the scenes in a restaurant, you'll appreciate that a certain amount of steam is let off when you think you're out of earshot of the general public.

There are times as a mystery shopper you feel sorry for those members of staff you are testing and this was one of those times. My sympathy lasted all of twenty minutes when Hannah returned to our table having visited the toilets downstairs (always a report requirement, that) no longer giggling but looking somewhat taken aback. My very attractive thirty-year-old sister, who was never short of male attention, had been approached by one of the staff members as she had made her way down the corridor. He had started to chat her up and when she had laughingly brushed him off by flashing her diamond ring at him and saying she had just had a baby, the man had responded by grabbing her around the waist purring, 'Oh my god, I can't believe a baby has come out of this beautiful body . . .' I don't think my sister even made it to the loo, she was back upstairs and telling all as soon as she could wriggle free.

Hannah laughed it off, she's built of tough stuff, but as soon as I got home I called the mystery-shopping company to report the incident. You're always supposed to run complaints past the mystery-shopping company first, rather than contact the company you are reporting on as you would in a genuine situation, and I never knew what steps they took. I was told to complete my report as normal but without any reference to what was at best entirely inappropriate behaviour towards my sister. I'd react very differently if I had my time again. We were somehow convinced back then that it was all right, but it absolutely wasn't.

It's hard to imagine now, so massive was the transition, but when I first joined Thomas Pink there was no voice-mail and no email. It suited my abilities pretty well since I had never worked in an office before so my computer literacy was basic.

One morning, every single one of the lines on the anti-quated telephone switchboard started to ring at almost exactly the same time. I started to answer each line, one by one, and it became clear every call was about the same thing.

'Oh hello, is that Thomas Pink? Can I order a pair of those pink wellies on Richard and Judy?'

'You know those wellies on the telly, do they come in a size 3?'

'Good morning, I've just seen a pair of pink Wellington boots I know my daughter would love . . .'

'Where can I get a pair of your pink boots, where is my nearest Thomas Pink?'

'Hello, I was in a Thomas Pink yesterday and they didn't have any of those boots on Richard and Judy?'

And so it went on.

As I failed hopelessly to keep up with the number of calls coming through, my boss came rushing down the corridor to see what was going on. As we stood there debating what to do, the telephone looking as if it might explode, suddenly there was silence. Every single one of the flashing red lights went out and the system went silent. Dead.

Nobody knew that Richard and Judy had their hands on the exclusive pink Wellington boots, and what Richard and Judy couldn't possibly have known was that they weren't even on sale in our stores. The tiny two-person marketing department at Thomas Pink head office was as taken by surprise as I was, because the pink boots were limited edition made solely for the forthcoming Cheltenham racing festival which the company was sponsoring.

Once the system gave up the ghost and I went off to make myself a cup of tea, I picked up my mobile to find a text message from my sister Hannah at home with baby Phoebe:

'Watching Richard and Judy. Love your pink wellies! Can you please get me a pair of size 4s? Xx'

Those pink boots sold out instantly at Cheltenham and were quickly put into production and shipped out to our stores soon after.

Meanwhile, back at HQ things were looking up, the marketing department hired a new assistant and the green light was given for a snazzy new telephone system complete with voicemail.

CHAPTER SIX

The Dorothy Perkins Mules

t wasn't only Thomas Pink who faced change. The Internet was taking off in the early noughties and brands were having to employ new staff or outsource to create a company website. Having a beautiful website was one thing; selling the goods on it was quite another. While Internet-based shops such as As Seen On Screen (ASOS) trail-blazed the concept of twenty-four-hour shopping from the comfort of your own home, the more dyed-in-the-wool brands took baby steps towards this new uncharted territory. Many shops, such as H&M, Zara and Harrods, had a website where you could scroll through products but weren't actually able to purchase online.

There were those who doubted the Internet as a medium for the sale of clothes and shoes. Their argument was that shoppers wanted to feel and try garments, and poor-quality pictures on a computer screen would never cut it. Was it any better than looking at clothes in a catalogue? Initially this was a valid point, as colour, fabrics and fit were poorly represented and photos took forever to download. Coupled with the delay of waiting for an order to arrive, possibly not being in to receive it and then potentially having to send it back with all the costs involved, wasn't it all just too much of a hassle?

Johnnie Boden himself admits to having doubted that 'middle-class women will get into this Internet thing'. Clearly he changed his mind.

Educated at Eton and then Oxford, Johnnie Boden started his career working as a stockbroker in the City. He hated it and after five years he decided to launch his own mail-order business. Boden launched in 1991 with eight hand-drawn menswear products. As it was lean times, friends from the City were called upon to model for Boden, and the decision was taken to associate the brand closely to his own identity and lifestyle to differentiate it from other rival brands. As Boden explained to the BBC in March 2014: 'The clothing market is very saturated and you need everything you can summon to make yourself seem different.'

Womenswear was quickly added to the Boden offering, and by 1996 they launched a childrenswear range too. Boden soon became the go-to brand for 'yummy mummies' all over the country.

The first I heard of it was when Clare and my sister, Hannah – both west Londoners – went to a Boden sale in the heart of yummy mummy territory, Chiswick. Both had got married and had babies before any of my other friends and so they were my only point of reference to baby stuff. Clare, I suspected, was using her daughter Jessica as an excuse for shopping with a company that did pretty party dresses for mother and child. As a fashion victim, it wasn't my sort of thing, but I could see that Boden was well made, versatile and classy. Perhaps this was the problem: Boden was too sophisticated for my H&M-led style.

Boden was the antithesis of Carrie Bradshaw running around New York with her knickers in her clutch bag. Never trend-led, it was all about the Breton stripe T-shirt, the cosy colourful knit and the school-run friendly chino. The fabrics Boden use are good quality and the design classic. Classy rather than brassy probably sums it up best. So popular is this particular aesthetic that the word 'Boden' has become an adjective, especially in parts of London where the label became something of a uniform: 'Oh, she's very Boden'. Never quite as cheap as you might hope, but with an almost constant 20 per cent promotion to be had, mums on the run couldn't get enough of it, the only problem being that you inevitably bump into others wearing the same clothes, my idea of a nightmare.

(I remember venturing out shopping in a lovely new print dress from Gap on the first warm day of the year. I had bought it right at the start of the spring season as my mum pointed out it was so pretty it would sell out if I waited for good weather. Within fifteen minutes of stepping out of the front door I had bumped into two other people wearing the exact same dress – both older, bigger and frankly not quite as Sienna Miller as I had imagined myself to look. The lesson there is to approach high-street prints with caution – a Marks and Spencer floral tea dress, for example, will be available to women all over the country. I've seen it happen with two Debenhams polka-dot prom dresses at one wedding, and at another a guest who showed up in the same frock from Coast as the bridesmaids. My sister has a friend who once went to IKEA in a yellow sweatshirt and was repeatedly mistaken for a member of staff, but that's a whole different story.)

Boden launched their website in 1999 and what had started as a little mail-order business was suddenly the natural successor to the Freemans catalogue. Unlike Freemans, which could be found in most houses when I was a child, Boden has a very strong British middle-class identity which was simultaneously its USP and its downside. The 'Oh, she's very Boden' observation is not always entirely complimentary.

Curiously, the target audience is twenty-five-to-fifty-year-olds, which covers young single working women to grandmothers. Delve further, though, and it seems that Boden knows its 'bull's-eye' customer to be thirty-five-year-old women with children, which is who the collections are designed for today. They're also mindful that these former working women will still want to look attractive and feminine if they return to work. This is where the slightly (only very slightly) more frivolous pieces come in: the fifties-style dresses, the kitten heels and the cashmere.

It's true that when a Boden catalogue is sitting there on the kitchen table it's impossible not to flick through it, but actually go on the website? Not so much. And yet 90 per cent of Boden's sales are made online. Many high-street retail outlets who sent out a catalogue to mail-order customers gradually stopped this practice when the Internet took over – glossy brochures are costly to produce after all – Thomas Pink was a good example of this. But others did not. H&M continued to send out catalogues several times a year, as did Liberty and Harrods. Given the enormity of its offering, the Boden catalogues that appear through your door are small and choice. And don't expect them to stop anytime soon, because if an item is removed from the catalogue its sales reportedly drop by 60 per cent.

As company websites became more and more integral to the success of a business, so mystery shopping inevitably broadened to include research focusing on this area. Assignments involved assessing their ease of use, speed and quality. There was rarely any fee – after all you didn't even have to get out of bed to do this kind of work – but you nearly always got to keep the purchases. I gradually earned the whole ten series of *Friends* on DVD that way.

*

It was in 2003 at my dad's surprise sixtieth birthday party that my brother brought his new girlfriend to meet the family. Christophe, the most laid back of the three of us, is also more secretive than Hannah and me, an understandable result of having two older sisters who overshare. Tall (at six foot three, way taller than my dad much to the amusement of both) and handsome, with a charming and flirtatious manner that he owed more to our dad than his height, Christophe played his cards close to his chest when it came to his personal life and didn't subject girlfriends to his family very often. Quite right too: I wouldn't want to have had to meet Hannah and me for the first time either. We do *know* how to behave, but it doesn't take much for us to dissolve into hysteria, rendered unable to speak, even to explain our rudeness.

Luckily, Lucy is the eldest of four so she gets it. That evening at the surprise barbecue in the garden, she charmed us all, and if she had felt nervous meeting the family, she didn't show it. For all her big blue-eyed girlyness, there was a steely ambition that Lucy could pull out of nowhere when needed.

Right at the beginning of her career, just out of university and not too sure what she wanted to do, Lucy had applied for a job at *Drapers* magazine. She arrived to find she would have to go through the horror that is the group interview.

I've never been to a group interview but I did do a group audition for drama school once and it was terrifying, an effective method of separating the wheat from the chaff, that's for sure – I was the chaff.

Lucy sits on a chair in a circle of about twenty-five candidates all up for the same job.

'Now, we would like you to tell us the thing you are most proud of,' says one of the interviewers.

While I would have been out of there, Lucy, on the other hand, is one of those people you can see leafing through the back history in her brain at break-neck speed.

The first candidate (poor sod) starts: 'I did a bungee jump when I visited Australia and I was really scared of heights . . .'

Lucy would be elegantly stifling a yawn if she isn't concentrating so hard on recalling her own proud story.

Second candidate: 'I did a bungee jump too, in America—'

'Sorry,' the interviewer interrupts. 'Can you think of something different please?'

There are twenty-four proud moments to go and Lucy is the last in the circle. Not only has she to come up with her own proud moment, it has to be sufficiently different from the rest – yikes.

' . . . and we raised five thousand pounds for the charity so it was a really proud moment for me,' finishes candidate number twenty-four.

Lucy clears her throat and her eyes dart around the assembled flushed candidates all of whom look like they wished they'd never come today.

'So, erm, Lucy is it?' The interviewer looks down at her clipboard. 'Yes, Lucy what has been your proudest achievement?'

Lucy exhales and says, 'I suppose it's losing all the weight really . . .'

'Oh? How much did you lose?' asks the interviewer.

'Well,' says Lucy getting into her stride, 'I was a size twenty. I could fit three of me into my old jeans now.'

You can hear a pin drop in that room because this is a genuinely impressive achievement, and everyone is trying really hard not to be caught checking Lucy out. Becoming aware she has a captive audience, Lucy crosses one long lean high-heel-booted leg over the other.

'Did you do Weight Watchers or something?' asks someone from the circle.

Lucy fills them in on how she lost the six stone, the tips she learnt along the way and what drove her to get there.

When she finally pauses for breath, the interviewer says, 'Stand up, then. Give us a twirl.'

And Lucy being Lucy goes bright red but gives them a twirl. It's not every day you give a twirl in an interview.

But then, it's not every day you completely fabricate a story about battling obesity to get a job.

Lucy won the advertising executive job at *Drapers*, and by the time she met my brother two years later, had been promoted to advertising manager. When we met her that balmy evening in August 2003 she was a willowy, very slim size 10. And she always had been.

Lucy was every bit as fascinated by fashion as I was and we hit it off. When one day she mentioned to my dad that she needed someone to write brand advertorials for *Drapers*, Dad suggested I might be good at it. Before I had time to huff and puff and remonstrate about knowing nothing about advertising, I was thrown in at the deep end interviewing and writing about all sorts of brands and products, from Miss Sixty to Ben Sherman, Triumph lingerie to Refrigiwear coats. I loved writing about fashion again and it proved to be a lucrative string to my bow.

I was in the unique position of working for the head office of one clothing brand, writing promotional pieces for various others and mystery-shopping reports for still more. On one day I worked a Thomas Pink shift in the morning, rushed up to Carnaby Street to interview the manager at Ben Sherman about their new shirt collection and then on the way home carried out a mystery-shopping assignment to another leading shirt retailer. I had my finger in so many retail pies, I was running out of fingers, but as long as the pies were in plentiful supply, I welcomed it.

When Thomas Pink was sold to LVMH (Louis Vuitton Moët Hennessy, the parent company of Donna Karan, Kenzo, Celine, Loewe, Dior, Givenchy, Guerlain, Veuve Cliquot and many more), I suddenly became more aware of the luxury market to which we were now linked. As staff we were lucky enough to start being invited to 'friends and family' sales which were past season or sample sales offering goods at up to 80 per cent off. I love a bargain and was always up for a sale, but I'd never been able to afford designer goods so this was a whole new ball game. I'd called Clare, who would miraculously find childcare at the drop of a hat, and she and I would happily wait in a slow-moving queue down some back street in Kensington until we were finally let in and let loose on the piles of stuff.

My first experience of such a thing was at a Christian Dior shoe sale. Strangely, perhaps because I went during office hours, there was hardly anyone there and so I took my time browsing around the warehouse picking out shoes, trying them on, chopping and changing before finally deciding upon a gorgeous pair of black strappy heels a size too small. Most importantly they only set me back £40. This gave me totally the wrong impression of what a high-end sample sale is really like. At the next, I was not prepared at all.

This time the sale was held in the Celine store itself on Bond Street. Clare and I showed up with our serious shopping heads on, which was just as well as the shop was full of hardcore fashionistas. Clare picked up a pair of classic black leather heels and tried them on. This was an excellent call because classic means it'll get plenty of wear. It's not unusual for sample sales to either be full of model sizes (too small in the clothes, too big in the shoes) or packed to the rafters with out-there stuff that nobody wanted, you know the sort of thing, almost anything in lime green and items with peculiar embellishment.

As Clare checked out her reflection in the mirror, she noticed a petite elegant lady, with shiny black hair dressed in an expensive looking skirt suit, who was also checking out the shoes and standing far too close for comfort. This lady didn't make eye contact and didn't avert her gaze from the shoes, whether they were on Clare's feet, in her hands or under one arm. Half an hour later, as Clare meandered from shoe rack to shoe rack, arms full of shoes she may or may not buy, the small smart lady still had her eye on the prize. There was a moment when feeling herself about to drop some of the shoes, Clare set them down so she could adjust her grip.

There was a blur of skirt suit and black shiny hair as the small lady seized her opportunity and made a lunge for the stash. But Clare was small and quick too and, as she was more sensibly dressed for battle, she grabbed every single shoe back and moved swiftly away. Only Clare knows for sure whether she really wanted that particular shoe that day, but she's no fool: once she saw how much that lady wanted those shoes, Clare knew she had to have them. Pocket-sized Clare with her big green smiley eyes may look unthreatening, but as any good shop assistant knows, you shouldn't judge a customer on appearance alone. Clare went home with several pairs of shoes, including the coveted pair, and the smart lady called it a day at the door rather than following her home.

We ended up with, among other things, a pair of Loewe high-heeled sandals in the softest palest pink suede, far too impractical to actually wear on most days of the year. But that's the thing with designer sales: you make the effort to go, you queue to get in, you queue to try things on and you queue to pay for them, so you have to make it worth the effort. It's not quite the luxury experience the designer intended, but it's certainly rewarding.

The next thing I knew I was being asked to report on that very same designer experience I had lusted after. To be considered for the luxury brands, I had to fill out another questionnaire and send in a full-length photograph of myself. This may sound slightly dodgy in terms of recruitment, but more often than not you sign up to these mystery-shopping companies on the strength of a few details about yourself, your shopping habits and a passport-sized photograph. It stands to reason that if they are going to send you into a shop in Knightsbridge selling watches for several thousand pounds, the company needs to know you will look the part. Primark hot pants and flip-flops from the supermarket may cut it, but why take the risk?

I was accepted (in my Zara dress and Dune shoes) as a 'high-end shopper' and started to carry out assignments to all sorts of expensive, intimidating shops. Bags costing well into the thousands, shoes you'd give your right eye for, jewels whose sparkle was hypnotising. Care is taken to not use the same shopper in the same branch for some time, as many of these brands are very exclusive. The fees reflect this. You can't feel overwhelmed by the prices of the goods you're discussing and – just like real life – it can feel embarrassing having to back out without making a purchase at the end of the visit. I was an actress so it wasn't hard for me to play the part of someone in the market for spending thousands of pounds on their wardrobe. You put the costume on and get into character and by the time you walk through the door you're convincing. Besides, why wouldn't I be someone with huge amounts of cash to spare?

The service was usually excellent and I lost count of the times I felt perilously close to splashing out on a luxury item I had no hope of being able to afford. I usually made a point of accessorising with at least one designer item when carrying out these high-end assignments, because apart from anything else it gave me the confidence to see it through.

Inevitably, though, there have been occasions when my preparation hasn't been as thorough as it could have been.

One day, after a busy morning shift at Thomas Pink, fingers raw from having helped the marketing department to tie ribbons around eighty cufflink boxes for a VIP customer evening at the Jermyn Street store that evening, I headed up to Oxford Street for an afternoon of mystery-shopping assignments. You don't get your expenses back for these visits, so I made sure I had several to carry out in one area to maximise the cost of the travel card.

First on my list was a very exclusive shoe shop, beloved of the rich and famous. My mission was to enquire about new shoes for a gala dinner. I peered into the shop window and tried hard not to salivate at the array of gorgeous red-carpet styles, all sparkling and displayed to their best advantage, and every single one representing a huge chunk – if not all – of my monthly paycheque.

And then I noticed my reflection in the glass. Oh dear. Perhaps I could pretend that my tired eyes were due to my jet-setting lifestyle, not from having been up since six o'clock. Perhaps I could describe my hair as 'windswept', but it looked nothing like the blown-out hairstyles of the shoppers and assistants within. But worst of all was what I was wearing on my feet. I was going into this temple of elegant sophistication, a place where the very finest, most delicate and beautifully crafted shoes were sold, wearing a pair of mules I bought for £15 in the Dorothy Perkins sale. I had two choices: I could either give up and go home, or I could tough it out and project such an aura of confidence and entitlement that my outfit would seem as if it came from Gucci, my shoes from Prada. I am not a quitter, so with a deep breath I put on my game face. Toughing it out it is.

Smiling grandly at the huge security guard on the door, I went into character: 'wealthy successful businesswoman who is so high-flying she doesn't have time to look in a mirror'. It seemed to work, or possibly the members of staff were so good at their jobs that they turned a blind eye to my mock suede shoes. Part of my assignment was to check whether or not the shop assistants acknowledged me within thirty seconds of arrival and approached me with an offer to help within five minutes. All was well. The assistant was smiley and attentive and was happy to recommend a selection of jaw-droppingly stunning shoes. She showed me to a plush seat and offered a glass of champagne to sip while I waited for her to return with the shoes I selected to try on.

I flicked through the store's brochure, page after page of fabulous styles. I tried to keep the expression on my face neutral as inside I started to feel a little depressed. The shoes were all so gorgeous, but well out of the price range of a struggling actor, mystery shopper and part-time receptionist. When the assistant returned with the shoes, she gave me another friendly smile as she settled herself at my feet. 'Have you got the day off to go shopping?'

I slipped back into character. 'Sadly not. I'm working today. I was supposed to be nipping out for a sandwich and then I remembered this very dull gala dinner I have coming up. I desperately need some new shoes for it.'

'Ah, I see. Well, we have some gorgeous new styles just in. I'm sure you'll find something today.'

The first pair of shoes was carefully taken from their layers of tissue paper inside the box. The smell of fine leather wafted towards me. Up close the shoes were so beautifully made, so perfectly proportioned, that I almost forgot to breathe. I go to take off my shoes . . . and then I remembered: they're the Dorothy Perkins mules and, compared to the delicate high heels that the assistant was offering me, it's as if they belonged to a different, less-evolved species of footwear. With a sly movement disguised as an elegant attempt to keep my knees together, both ankles angled away from the assistant who is kneeling on the floor, I slipped off the offending shoes so the sole – which has DP emblazoned on it – was turned away.

But over the next half hour or so, what had begun as a teeth-clenchingly awkward exercise in pretending to be a different person became more like one of the dressing-up sessions I enjoyed as a child. I tried on five or six pairs of shoes, each more gorgeous than the last, discussing the pros (so many) and cons (very few) of each style, and lapping up the compliments from the friendly assistants. Yes, I thought, as I took another sip of champagne. This type of shopping is clearly made for me.

'I love your top, by the way, it's really unusual.' The voice of the shop assistant interjected.

'Oh thanks! Yes, would you believe it's T—' I stopped. I'd almost blown my cover by suggesting that the lovely assistant head down to Tesco's to get herself one before they all sold out. 'It's . . . it's . . . terrible – I can't remember for the life of me who it's by . . .'

Thankfully, the assistant didn't offer to check the label of my top. Before I dug myself deeper into the hole, I made my excuses and left.

One assignment down, two more to go. It was going to be a long afternoon . . .

The relationships between fashion designers and the stars who wear their clothes on the red carpet and magazine covers was nothing new, and the greatest ever collaboration was arguably that of Audrey Hepburn and Hubert de Givenchy that started way back in the 1950s when they hooked up for some of her finest films – *Breakfast at Tiffany's*, *Sabrina* and *Funny Face* to name but three. The partnership created a style icon, although neither could have known that then, and a style that would never date. Shortly before she died, Hepburn gave back twenty-five of her dresses to her old friend Givenchy, and one by one he is distributing them to museums all over the world.

In an interview with *Vanity Fair*, Givenchy describes what Hepburn was wearing when they first met: 'This very thin person with beautiful eyes, short hair, thick eyebrows, very tiny trousers, ballerina shoes, and a little T-shirt. On her head was a straw gondolier's hat with a red ribbon around it that said VENEZIA.' Clearly she already had her own very recognisable sense of style, but combined with the expertise of Hubert de Givenchy, as Dreda Mele Givenchy's former 'directrice' and now general manager for Armani says, 'They were made for each other.'

From Elizabeth Hurley and her borrowed Versace dress onwards, awards season, which starts with the Golden Globes in January and ends with the Academy Awards in March, was as much about who wore what as who won what, every ceremony a conveyor belt of borrowed gowns and jewellery with the attendees hoping to be top of the best-dressed lists in the morning. Get the dress wrong and you could get attention for all the wrong reasons, and it didn't matter if you won an award or not. Everybody remembers Bjork's swan dress and Sharon Stone's inspired choice of her husband's white shirt tucked into a long satin skirt, but does anyone recall who won the award for best actress on those occasions?

For a few years running my brother had worked with the BAFTA production team responsible for the coverage that went out on the BBC. Each year the footage of the stars arriving and making their way into the Royal Opera House was slightly more lingering, until finally in 2007 the producer decided to have an additional bod on the carpet questioning nominees about what they were wearing. That person was me. While my brother was at one end of the carpet in the freezing cold drizzle making informed chat about production values and exactly how much hard work goes into preparing for the role of a lifetime, I was at the other, asking the equally chilly and scantily clad celebs who they were wearing.

Not everyone is pleased to hear that question, and while I'd imagined the least you could do is name-check the designer who has kindly lent you the thousand pound dress on your back, for some this is asking too much. That night I spoke to so many beautiful actresses in show-stopping gowns but the ones who stuck out for their grace and star quality were Dames Judi Dench and Helen Mirren, both of whom looked exquisite. The actress Helen McCrory, who told me she had been breast-feeding right up until she squeezed into her dress, and her husband Damian Lewis were gorgeous as were Anne-Marie Duff and James McAvoy. Both couples seemed to appreciate the moment for what it was and didn't make judgements on those hired to ask the sartorial questions those at home wanted to know the answers to. Somewhere in the dark recesses of my sister's Sky News email account, there are pictures she unearthed the day after those BAFTAS. There I am, microphone clutched in blue hand, producer's urgent voice in my ear and desperation etched on my face as I try to catch the attention of actors Daniel Craig and Jake Gyllenhaal, looking mighty fine in their slim fitting tuxedos and striding purposefully on straight past me. So near and yet so far . . .

There are worse ways to earn money than hanging with the beautiful and famous, whether it is on the red carpet or trying on designer shoes in glamorous and exclusive environments. However, when all is said and done you are still merely trying on the lifestyle, imagining how it might be if this was your reality. Could these beautiful shoes change your life for the better? As you reluctantly make your excuses and say your goodbyes without making a purchase, as surely even wealthy people do sometimes, it's no different to any other shopping trip when you risk not only your own disappointment but that of the shop assistant who loses out on her commission. On those mystery-shopping assignments that involve spending a lot of money, sometimes £1,000 or more, it's a challenge not to walk out of the store with a bit of a swagger: having been on the receiving end of attentive customer service and amassed several colourful branded bags that scream 'Look at me, I can afford to shop here, I've got sophisticated style!' can go to your head somewhat.

Luckily, many shops say you can try their products on at home in the so-called 'cooling off period', so that's exactly what I do before sending them back to the market research companies. It's surprising how much fun doing the hoovering in your underwear and a pair of fabulous shoes worth £450 can be. It's the little things. My nightmare scenario of accidentally leaving the very expensive items on the tube has only happened once, and thankfully I was given the benefit of the doubt and reimbursed the money anyway. When you're earning as little as £8 per report, the last thing you need is to be out of pocket by £150 on your credit card.

Parking tickets are not so easy to get out of and I have a terrible history with these. While some assignments can be far quicker and easier than you anticipate, there are others that take a complicated turn and before you know it you have overrun your parking payment and there is very little you can do other than sweat it out. I would hate to add up all the parking tickets and weigh them up against what I have actually earned over the years. There's no question that, as jobs go, mystery shopping has at times been a costly path for me to take. Let's do the sums on an average assignment:

Visit to *insert brand here* in Richmond
Fee £6.50
+
Allowable spend for item to keep (for which you will be reimbursed) £10
= £16.50

Parking expenses £2.00
+
Actual spend after being genuinely convinced by persuasive assistant £79
-
£16.50 total
=
£64.50 out of pocket (although extremely fabulous skirt now in wardrobe).

Conclusion: it certainly helps to be interested in fashion and shopping and good service, but it can also be your downfall.

It's undoubtedly a very fortunate thing that those assignments involving seriously expensive items such as jewellery and watches don't require purchases. Sitting in a pricey jeweller's on Bond Street with a cold drink kindly brought by an affable assistant for whom nothing is too much trouble, while I admire the rose-gold watch on my wrist, is not the only time that the urge to grab my bag and make a run for the door has kicked in. The £8 fee would not be worth a trip to the police station and a possible court date, but it's interesting how often these thoughts take over. While the assistant rattles on about quality, after-sales care and matching items, I am on a beach in the Bahamas in my rose-gold watch, lying on a sun lounger with a cocktail on the go. It's escapism, really, not dissimilar to going to the cinema to watch a feel-good film.

Suspension of disbelief is a great thing and what you are constantly striving for in the theatre world. For example, one of my assignments was to shop for engagement rings, which I'd never done before. It was with a sense of trepidation that I approached a series of visits to independent diamond boutiques. Not only did my superstitious side give me the feeling that it might be tempting fate to try on and discuss diamond rings, my fiancé and my 'forthcoming nuptials', but sitting in an upmarket jewellery shop specialising in diamond rings just around the corner from where a relatively new boyfriend lived gave me the jitters. At that stage in our relationship I hadn't even told him about the mystery-shopping side of my life (some mystery shoppers keep their work completely secret from family members, so seriously do they take the mystery part of their role), so if he happened to walk past the shop I'd have had a job explaining my presence there that day – not to mention having my cover blown! Having said that, dare I say I surprised myself by quite enjoying it? And I picked myself out a lovely ring.

Towards the end of the twentieth century and well into the noughties, the importance of designer labels and their branding was taken to ever greater heights by personalities from the hip-hop scene and the phenomenon of the WAGS – wives and girlfriends of sports (mainly football) stars. Logomania took over. Wearing your wealth on your sleeve, no matter how brazen – pink Juicy Couture tracksuits, red Louboutin soles and even diamond teeth decorations – replaced fur and jewels as status symbols. In addition to the Burberry check, the Louis Vuitton, Chanel and Gucci logos that had been synonymous with exclusivity suddenly became naff, gradually symbolising a lack of taste rather than the epitome of it.

The 'It' bag of the season was reliant on the mega rich being photographed with it on their arm at every available opportunity, Victoria Beckham and her Hermès Birkin was one example, Mulberry's Gisele, named after the Brazilian supermodel, another. Victoria reportedly had several Birkins in various colours so she could match the must-have accessory with whichever outfit she was wearing. At several thousand pounds a pop this was not an accessible trend and eventually, as with the logos, there was a backlash. The It bag found itself the focus of satire in an episode of *Sex and the City*, and suddenly it had a new label, that of vulgarity.

Despite the trademarking of such logos as the Gucci 'double Gs' and the Chanel 'double Cs', the demand for the so-called 'bling' look from those who couldn't afford the real thing meant a boom in the counterfeit industry with fakes becoming ever harder to distinguish from the genuine articles. Even though I'd been buying knockoffs as far back as the eighties, when I'd bought cheap sunglasses on the beach in the south of France, nothing could prepare me for the lengths people would go to for Louis Vuitton pieces.

It was during a peach of a job filming in France, for the made-for-television film *Last Days of a Princess*, that I found myself staying in the very smart Hotel Regina on the Rue de Rivoli, opposite the Tuileries in Paris.

Those hours when I wasn't on set, I was hanging out, mostly window shopping and using my per-diem to buy croissants and Chanel lipsticks. I even managed to carry out a mystery-shopping visit to a museum while I was there.

I had friends who worked in Thomas Pink's Paris branch, so one sunny afternoon I headed out to say hello. On the way I was inevitably distracted by the myriad boutiques and shops, slowing down as I approached the very grand branch of Louis Vuitton. I decided to have a quick look when I heard an urgent voice beckoning me from the hedgerow. I looked over my shoulder to see a diminutive Chinese lady with a big smile. She told me she desperately wanted a Louis Vuitton wallet but the staff in the shop would not serve her. I immediately felt sorry for her and asked her why she had been treated so badly, however my question was studiously ignored. The lady pounced on my sympathetic expression and shoved a wad of notes in my hand telling me to buy her a wallet 'or anything' with the money and she would be there waiting for me. She shooed me off, all the while chattering on about the staff wanting to serve a 'nice blond lady'.

Don't get me wrong, I knew this was something out of the ordinary, but I didn't think I was doing anything illegal myself. The fact was, I was intrigued. I decided to go through with it.

Unlike the mystery shop reports I carry out where I seem to go successfully incognito, the staff in this Paris branch of Louis Vuitton were immediately on to me. Although I don't know why, I wondered if there was CCTV outside and they had seen the clandestine deal take place. Accustomed as I am to being able to pull the wool over shop assistants' eyes with my public-school accent and arsenal of aloof mannerisms, the Parisian insouciance threw me and I started to feel a bit uncomfortable. I could feel myself breaking into a sweat. Possibly it was the huge amounts of cash stuffed into my bag that did it.

The member of staff ultimately let me get away with it – impeccable customer service winning through – but I could tell she was unconvinced and very reluctant to sell me anything, no matter how small. I left the shop with half a mind to make off with the Louis Vuitton wallet and let the Chinese lady sit in the bushes all day. However, she was on to me the minute I left the shop and so I dutifully handed the swag over to her. If I expected some kind of reward or thanks I was deluded. Not a bit of it. I didn't even get the big smile, she grabbed her wallet and was gone in a puff of smoke.

The Paris shoot was the second time I had been part of a production focusing on Princess Diana, the first being when I provided the voiceover for a television documentary. A few years earlier, I had sat down in the sound proof booth at the recording studio awaiting the film on the screen to resume playing so the director could cue me in. I got comfortable, checked out the script, secured my headphones and looked up at the screen to find myself staring at an image of my dad paused in mid-sentence. Seen as a bit of an expert on the royals and always happy to give his opinion, Dad had been interviewed for the very same documentary.

The more time I spent being introduced to, talked through and trying on designer collections, the more knowledge I acquired about the luxury market and the different designers available. Although I didn't have a preference for designer labels, I did appreciate the craftsmanship involved. But also, the exposure I had to the very expensive world of Bond Street and Sloane Street gave me a unique insight into the increasing ability the high-street stores had for offering impressive imitations. It's a great game to leave a swanky West End department store empty-handed to then cross over the road and go straight into H&M, Cos or & Other Stories and unearth duplicate items for a fraction of the price. The fabrics are dubious and often the rails and rails of stock are creased and squished together, unlike a high-end store where everything is beautifully merchandised, but that's half the fun.

As I signed on with more high-end mystery-shopping research companies, the perks improved. I was getting regular expensive haircuts, cosmetics and meals out. I was also gaining an inordinate amount of dog food and travel sickness pills, neither of which were any use to me at all.

The up-and-down nature of my work, and consequently my income, meant I couldn't often afford an expensive piece, but after my first television acting paycheque arrived I went straight to Harrods to buy a fabulous red figure-hugging dress by D&G.

On an evening out with my school friends Sara and Hannah, who was heavily pregnant, we went to the Anchor and Hope gastro pub on The Cut in Waterloo. It was a warm summer's evening. I filled them in on the latest drama of my long-distance relationship with a Dubai-based man I'd met at a wedding. Evenings like this, spent with two of my favourite people, were the most fun and happened not often enough for my liking. We said our goodbyes and agreed to meet up again as soon as possible, before Hannah gave birth.

How fast time flew. I'd known these two since we were eleven and now one of us was about to become a mum. As I walked back through Waterloo station to catch my train back to Clapham Junction, my mobile phone rang. It was my mum, and she was asking if I was on my way over. On my way over? No, I wasn't, I was at Waterloo station, on my way home, why would she ask that? Why was she calling me this late?

I didn't want her to say anything else, I wanted her to say it could wait until tomorrow and she'd speak to me in the morning. Except it couldn't wait, I knew that from her quiet and frightened voice. I knew something was terribly wrong and that standing there on my own in the middle of Waterloo station, surrounded by people rushing past to catch the last train, I was about to hear the news that would turn all of our lives upside down.

My dad had cancer, and it was in the pancreas, one of the trickiest to diagnose and one of the most difficult to treat. The prognosis wasn't good; it never is for this type of cancer. My dad was rarely ill; he was young and fit and healthy for his age. He'd had some weight loss, which had prompted people to say how well he looked, and a few aches and pains, but aside from that he hadn't had any symptoms.

I found the fact that my dad had cancer hard to believe.

My dad wasn't supposed to get cancer, he still worked, he swam several times a week, he liked to joke about becoming old and annoying at a point way, way in the future. He had years left in him, I thought, though actually I hadn't thought about his death much at all. He was only sixty-two and I was still mucking about with different boyfriends and jobs as if we'd all be around for ever.

Suddenly, I felt like an adult. We needed a plan otherwise how would we deal with this unthinkable thing? We had to think positively; we had no choice. Dad agreed. He felt really quite well, so he continued to write his weekly column for the *Sunday Mirror* for as long as the chemotherapy would allow. He also agreed to edit his old friend and colleague Alastair Campbell's diaries for publication. It was a massive job and Dad was determined to see it through. We arranged a family trip to Paris and focused on being together and having as much fun as possible. It simply wasn't conceivable to imagine life without this man, the life and soul of our party, so we didn't.

I packed as much into my schedule as possible so I didn't have time to dwell on things. We told very few people, which was how Dad wanted it, and it helped to keep things as normal as possible.

Dad died on a Monday morning in July, eighteen days before his sixth-fourth birthday. He had fought what had, at times, seemed like a hopeless battle against his illness. It's an awful disease, and although he lived for thirteen months after his diagnosis and appeared quite well for some of that time, we always knew pancreatic cancer had one of the lowest survival rates, one that had not improved in over forty years. Sometimes I convinced myself that Dad would recover, but being larger than life wasn't enough.

There was talk of having time to prepare ourselves for losing him but I knew I couldn't do that. When you're savouring every moment left, it seems illogical to also try to make preparations for the immeasurable grief to come. Occasionally I sat in my car and howled at the unfairness of it all, still so much life left in him and he had only been grandfather to Hannah's daughter Phoebe for two years. It wasn't so much the thought of how much he had left to give to the world but rather how much I wanted to give to him. He would never meet any children I might have and that thought was unbearable to me. Like an idiot I had thought he would always be there and now we had run out of time.

Without even realising it, a door closed for me that day. I fell out of love with the acting profession. Or perhaps that had already happened and the loss of my dad, he who had inspired and encouraged me every step of the way, meant I felt it was time to start a new chapter without having to admit to him that my heart simply wasn't in it any more.

CHAPTER SEVEN

An Ivory Ralph Lauren Dress

Clapham Junction, which most people understandably assume to be in Clapham but is actually in Battersea, was becoming more expensive by the day, and while it maintained its eclectic mixture of pound shops and designer boutiques, takeaways and wine bars, property was ever more unattainable for young single people who would end up settling in nearby Tooting and Balham instead.

I was lucky, I had my lovely little flat with its (thankfully) small mortgage, my job at Thomas Pink was within walking distance (although walking took forty minutes so that was a rare occurrence) and Rich, ex-boyfriend and best male friend and sounding board, still lived around the corner.

It had never been a more exciting time to be a single girl about town. Exciting but treacherous. There was a great sense of camaraderie among those of us yet to get married and settle down: a group of people who could celebrate good news at the drop of a hat, as well as a reliable support network for when the lows struck.

The dating world had become more transient and cutthroat and it seemed that the New York lifestyle depicted in *Sex and the City* had found its way across the Atlantic. It was funny when we watched Carrie, Samantha, Miranda and Charlotte negotiate their route to forty via every known pitfall and dysfunctional relationship known to womankind. It didn't feel so funny when it was closer to home. Well, occasionally it did. Like when a friend of a friend was out with a date who failed to come back from the loo. She waited and waited because she knew he'd come back eventually to get his coat which was slung over the back of the chair. He didn't: he actually sacrificed his coat rather than return and she never heard anything of him again.

Living in the same flat I had bought with James, I had the good fortune to find in its hallways three brilliant people. Aaron, a former submariner, lived on the ground-floor. He was a terrific organiser and immediately took charge of the upkeep of the building. Sarah, a high-flying City girl with a penchant for feather boas, hats and straight-talking, lived on the first floor, and I was on the top. We shared a hallway and a front door, and this was how we discovered that Aaron had a new girlfriend, Cesca – in fact, this was how we all knew quite a lot about each other's lives. On warm summer evenings we would share cocktails and gossip on the stoop. It was an unusually friendly set up for a building in London, our very own sitcom. For Sarah and me it was an added bonus that after one too many glasses of wine we only had to crawl back up the stairs to get to our beds.

I was sad when first Sarah moved out of the first-floor flat and then Aaron and Cesca got married, had their daughter Paloma and moved to Kingston. I was rather lagging behind my closest friends, too, who by this time had carved out good careers for themselves with decent salaries, were selling flats for houses and getting married. It didn't overly bother me, however. I was going out a lot, meeting new people and travelling, and I always had some ridiculous escapade to regale. But the house in Battersea was never the same and I would find myself hiding in the corridor rather than having to make friends with the new people.

The residents of Clapham Junction were ever-changing but the area itself was slow to catch up, but catch up it did. The famous Arding and Hobbs, where I had bonded over a basque with my director friend Kerry, was now a Debenhams, although it was a listed building so not much had changed. Kerry herself had moved away from the area when she married but she made regular trips back to visit her old stomping ground. There weren't so many mobile phone shops as there once had been and so the days of carrying out three different mobile phone shop assignments in one afternoon were long gone. In their place were a L'Occitane, a Jamie Oliver's Recipease, a Body Shop and at least three trendy burger joints within two minutes of each other.

However, the biggest excitement of all was when the hoarding went up next to Debenhams and big red signs appeared, declaring that TK Maxx was on its way. Oh the joy! A TK Maxx within walking distance of my home! Things were looking up. I got straight on the phone to Kerry to tell her the good news.

I had first discovered outlet stores when visiting New York in the 1990s. TJ Maxx, as it is called in the States, first opened in Massachusetts in 1977 and was a low-key slightly down-at-heel store. TK Maxx first opened in Bristol in 1994 but it wasn't until the early noughties that it really took off in the UK, with branches springing up in local high streets sometimes alongside the very retailers whose slashed-price stock they were offering.

This supermarket-style shop with its 'Big Labels, Small Prices' strapline offers rail upon rail of clothes, merchandised in sizes rather than colour, and by type of garment rather than collections. No outfit suggestions here, you have to do all the hard work yourself. The designer bargains are sometimes available in a range of sizes but more often than not are one-offs in random sizes hence the 'When it's Gone, it's Really Gone' warning signs. If you are lucky a current season gem can be snapped up, but the challenge is to sift through the huge amount of lower quality goods produced by unheard-of brands, often manufactured by TK Maxx themselves. A lot of time, patience and a good eye for sizing and labels is the key to bagging a bargain. It's something of a skill and a challenge far more popular with women than men. Men tend to shop only when they need something, and they usually depend on tried and trusted labels and then buy in bulk.

Melanie Traub worked in luxury retail for twelve years before becoming chief commercial officer at flash-sale site Secret Sales. 'TK Maxx has great relationships with big brands worldwide,' she explains. 'They can take huge quantities of stock and can pay up front, however they pay low prices so some brands would rather go to flash sites and do regular sales every few months.'

For those smaller independent brands, whose product is so carefully merchandised and targeted, the prospect of it ending up in TK Maxx isn't an attractive one. Jodi Zervos, who runs the successful New Zealand boutique Merino Kids, which sells 100 per cent natural garments for babies and children, agrees. 'It's a tricky area to balance. Discount outlets are an option but you effectively sell to them at well below cost [price].' Jodi says they prefer to do it themselves because it is better money that way. Cost has to be considered, as well as the store versus cash flow versus new season stock.

Eric Musgrave, former editorial director of fashion bible *Drapers* magazine, points to leading online designer boutique Net-a-Porter, who launched the Outnet, their own outlet branch that presents their past season stock in a way that is still aesthetically pleasing and respects the brand's values, despite the slashed prices.

Holly Browne, Thomas Pink's supplier compliance coordinator, admits that the problem of what to do with large amounts of excess stock is a big problem for the fashion industry. Ideally the company wants to make money from their product but what to do with that product at the end of its life? That's the million-dollar question: no brand wants to be seen to have stock they can't sell, but it has to go somewhere.

'This is perhaps why,' Eric says, 'there are some international brands who will willingly sell their stock on to TK Maxx but won't allow it to be sold in their own country.' That's fair enough, there are plenty of actors who will happily take the money for commercials as long as they are only to be shown in other territories than where they live.

But TK Maxx seems to be an ever-more popular way of doing things, at least for those companies who don't have their own high-street presence. Alberta Ferretti, D&G,

Ralph Lauren, Chloè, Martin Miguela, Marc Jacobs and Versace can regularly be found at the Clapham Junction branch and often at incredible prices; a £1500 dress down to £499 is still a lot of money, but it's an undeniably amazing reduction.

The décor and layout of TK Maxx is stark, brightly lit and much of the stock can be found discarded on the floor – there is little attention paid to display. You'll notice TK Maxx branches don't have window displays at all, instead offering a view straight into the action. There is also no discernible customer service. You do not go to TK Maxx to be valued as a loyal customer or to experience fragrances at the counter and a scarf to cover your make-up in the fitting room.

'Our no-frills way of working helps us pass spectacular savings onto you [the customer]' we are told on the TK Maxx website, where the advice is to visit often to snap up the best pieces from some 50,000 items in store. With 10,000 new items arriving each week – from over 10,000 vendors in sixty countries – a high turnover of stock is ensured. TK Maxx is going from strength to strength and proving especially popular in times of recession. There are now over 260 stores in the UK alone.

The TK Maxx website launched in 2009. Although less successful than the high-street stores, it hosts so-called 'Flash Events' online, usually focusing on one designer at a time, offering larger quantities with a variety of sizes and where coveted labels such as Stella McCartney and

Pucci can often be picked up for less than half the original retail price.

If a designer boutique selling collections at full price is at the top, and outlet villages where the merchandise is always at sale prices is somewhere in the middle, then TK Maxx is a last-chance saloon for clothes that nobody wants. The TK Maxx clearance rail, then, is where clothes go to die. And it has to be said that often these garments look as if they have been used as dish rags before having the red price tag slapped on their labels. But if you're canny, this is where the real steals are found, usually because something has been sized incorrectly or has the wrong label attached. This is how I have found designer jeans by Ernest Sewn and a Woolrich jacket for less than a third of its retail price. If you can see past the torn and worn shirts and the knitwear of Christmases past, then you may just strike gold, but this takes time and stamina and a dedication to the cause.

I am in TK Maxx a lot. If it's good enough for Prince Harry, who was papped shopping in the Kensington High Street branch in 2013, then it's good enough for me. If I leave it longer than a week before checking out the stock, I have FOMO: Fear Of Missing Out. I once followed a woman around the shop floor of my local branch in the hope that she might change her mind about the handbag she had picked out which was now hanging on her toddler's pram. I am guilty of hiding covetable pieces in among the dross to allow me to return to buy it after my lunch hour when the snake-like queue has reduced. I don't do queues. It would have to be an exceptional item for me to stand behind many other people buying basketfuls of socks, slippers and oddly flavoured fudge.

∽

HOW TO SHOP AT TK MAXX

1. Keep an open mind. Don't set yourself up for disappointment. You are unlikely to find a pair of jeans if that's what you're specifically looking for, but you might well go home with something far more interesting if you widen the search. I have a Ralph Lauren piece, which looks suspiciously like a wedding dress fit for a slightly bohemian dreamy beach wedding. It is totally inappropriate for any other occasion I can think of, particularly in south London. I wasn't looking for a wedding dress when I bought it but how useful to have one on standby should one suddenly decide to get married on a beach at a moment's notice. More to the point it was £1,000 cheaper than the recommended retail price so it seemed rude not to.

2. It's obvious, but stick with classic shapes and timeless colours. You can't go wrong with a black trench (I got a D&G one in TK Maxx) but a newspaper print Galliano dress isn't going to necessarily cut it simply because Carrie wore a similar version in *Sex and the City* (yup, me again). Sometimes the reason the garment is living

out its days in a discount store is all too clear. If you find yourself thinking 'It's so fabulous but I just can't think where I'd wear it . . .' then that's probably because there simply isn't anywhere anyone would wear it. The deciding question for me, actually on any purchase I'm not 100 per cent sure about, is this: 'How would I feel if I bumped into someone I hadn't seen since school wearing this?'

3. Make sure you're signed up to their email updates, and log your sizes with them if possible. Designer underwear, tights and jeans are regular features in TK Maxx, and they are well worth spending the money on for the most perfect, comfortable flattering fit. There are very few things in life more uncomfortable than badly fitting jeans or underwear, other than maybe the scene in *Friends* where Rachel's new boyfriend arrives to take her on a date and she's wearing a wedding dress. You see, there's another reason why you should avoid having a wedding dress with no purpose in your wardrobe. You *will* at some point try it on and you *will* get caught.

4. TK Maxx, much as I love it, isn't always up to speed on size conversions from Italian and American into British. A common mistake is a US6 in the UK6 section rather than its correct home along with the size UK10s, and an Italian 42 is a UK10. If you don't try things on before you buy it can be very disappointing to get home and find you have the wrong size. I appreciate it's hard to tell the perfect size of anything just by looking at

it, but try it just in case. I have a pair of skinny jeans by Made in Heaven which cost £15 down from £150 because clearly the label was confusing everyone.

◦◦

The outlet village was conceived once again in the States, where it achieved relative success in the 1980s. It moved across the pond in 1995, when the McArthurGlen group opened Cheshire Oaks outlet village, the first of its kind in Europe. At Thomas Pink we opened our first outlet in Swindon, and further branches in York and Bicester were soon to follow. If you thought discount stores were only for students and those who can't afford designer prices, then think again. Years of writing the company newsletter and monitoring the celebrity count at Thomas Pink branches worldwide threw up Jeremy Clarkson, Jodie Kidd, Carol Vorderman and Elizabeth Hurley all shopping for shirts at the Bicester branch.

At Bicester Village (run by Value Retail, a rival to the McArthurGlen chain), which also opened in 1995, 65 per cent of their visitors are international tourists who are brought in by coach. In 2014, 9,800 tour buses took Chinese tourists from their hotels in London to grab a designer piece by Burberry, Jimmy Choo or Alexander McQueen for a far lower price than they could find back home. For the Chinese, Bicester Village is second only to Buckingham Palace on the list of places to visit.

Tara Sendell, who worked as social coordinator for Value Retail, was responsible for checking that all ten of their locations were on-brand and putting across the same message to the 6.3 million people who flock to this funny little mock-up of a New England town.

In fact, the impact of international shoppers on the UK retail industry as a whole was gaining momentum year on year. In particular, those Chinese visitors holidaying in Europe who made shopping sprees the focus of their trip were spending more money than travellers from any other nation. The pull? Not only the luxury goods available for far less than in China but also the British brands that had not yet made the transition to their own high street. There are now over fifty designer outlet villages in the UK and the first London Village opened in 2014. And yet, Paris was welcoming over ten times the number of visitors than London.

This was down to the Schengen Agreement, a collection of twenty-five countries that had done away with passport control at their common borders, and which the UK had chosen, perhaps wisely, to opt out of. Chinese travellers who wanted to travel freely to both the UK and the rest of Europe needed to apply for two visas, which was costly, complicated and time-consuming, and many were bypassing London as a result. So the 2014 government announcement that a review of the Schengen Agreement was underway was welcomed widely by British retailers. In July 2015 a new scheme was piloted: a shared visa application form creating a one-stop shop for Chinese visitors to the UK and Europe whether they were coming for business or pleasure.

Another side of Tara Sendell's work for Bicester Village was managing the information going out via their Chic Outlet Shopping social channels. Value Retail has only one village in each country where they have a presence, so tourists coming to Europe on shopping trips want to be able to plan their visits to include as many of the locations as possible. In order to do so they need to know exactly what is available and what promotions are happening and where. It is not unusual for visitors from Asia and the UAE to fly to the UK, Italy, France and Germany to shop in all the villages. Package deals include flights, hotels and coach trips. 'Even factoring in the cost of extra suitcases to stash all their purchases in, it works out cheaper because of the tax-free element, goods costing up to 60 per cent less and far wider brand availability than in their native country. It's a very attractive proposition,' explains Tara. 'Out-of-towners love them, it's a real coup and there are some people who really do travel to every single outlet village in Europe in one trip!'

At Bicester's designer outlet village today, it seems hard to imagine they are missing out on any international shoppers as coach after coach drops yet more bargain-hungry tourists off for the day. The car parks, the open-air village layout and the retail units themselves have expanded – they currently boast annual sales of £2,500 per square foot – and have the feel of a luxury boutique not dissimilar to their full-priced designer relatives on Bond Street. You don't get the bargain-basement feel of a TK Maxx or a Primark here; they want you to spend the whole day at the village so they've thought of almost everything in order to provide you with 'Quality, attention to detail and five-star service' which, according to the Bicester Village website, are 'the hallmarks of the Bicester Village shopping experience'.

To this end, they offer valet parking, hand cream in the toilets, a personal stylist, a children's play area, free Wi-Fi and a contemplation room. Ah yes, the contemplation room which, the website tells us simply, is 'located next to Dior'. So after you've spent a month's wages on last season's Christian Dior mustard yellow jacket in extra small because it'll be perfect once you've lost half a stone and well, it was 70 per cent off after all, you can nip next door to have a good think about what you've done.

You will probably find yourself lured out of your contemplations by the intoxicating smell coming from the crepe stall which is placed conveniently right in the middle of the village, so no matter where you are you will be drawn to it. When you arrive at the stall and make your choice you will then have to backtrack to find the end of the queue a half mile past all the shops. That's handy, another chance to walk past all the shops again and then another half an hour to window shop while you wait to be served. You realise you should have paid the

£15 for 'hands-free shopping', where your purchases are packed for collection later, which would have made the wait and the endless traipsing backwards and forwards up and down the promenade far less arduous. On a weekend or in end-of-season sale periods, the place is heaving. The average visitor spends three hours at Bicester Village and spends more than £500, which if you've also forked out for a local hotel is quite an outlay. But then naturally, this being destination shopping, the hotels are in on it too. You might be able to blag a lift in a swanky car to and from the hotel, who may send you off with a 10 per cent off discount card.

Bicester Village is home to high-end labels such as Moncler, Bonpoint, Ralph Lauren, Alexander McQueen, Dolce & Gabbana and Vivienne Westwood. Its offering is high end and the stock is largely decent because Bicester is where the brands send their excess stock first. Melanie Traub explains: 'Bicester is so competitive. [For brands] to keep their place there the less good, lower price stock will need to be sold elsewhere.' With over twenty-five years in fashion retail, twelve of them in the luxury market, Melanie is well versed in what does and doesn't sell. 'Bicester usually gets the stock first and then older stock or excess comes to the flash sites.'

When Bicester was new, Kevin Knox, a store designer who has worked for Thomas Pink and Hugo Boss, was asked to take a look around. Reporting back to Value

Retail, Kevin's immediate reaction was to wonder where all the cafes and restaurants were. Unlike any other mall or high street you might find yourself in, Bicester had just one outlet in which to sit, kick back and have a coffee and sandwich. With the number of units and the footfall, this was never going to cut it. If you visit Bicester now, you will find a Starbucks, a Villandry and a Carluccio's to name just three places to take time out from the dawdling hordes and to recharge your batteries before going back out there for round two. As of 2015, there was also a new railway line shuttling shoppers from London straight into Bicester Village twice an hour. Amazingly, this is the first new line in 100 years to link London with somewhere that isn't London.

Like TK Maxx, it's pot luck whether you come home with anything really good. Unlike TK Maxx, the outlet villages are destination shopping centres for which you tend to dedicate a whole day so it's almost unacceptable to come home empty-handed.

My first visit to Bicester Village was in my mystery shopper guise, and strangely, given the nature of mystery shopping, it was for Thomas Pink, the very company I worked for. When the retail operations department asked me to help them conduct a series of assignments to the branches outside London, I couldn't believe my luck – time out of the office spent sitting on trains, drinking coffee with a little bit of shopping in between. It hadn't occurred to me that within the confines of a working day, there would be precious little time to even stop for a sandwich.

As I sat on the empty train to Bicester that Monday morning, trying hard not to nod off, I looked over the report I was to complete. It was the standard enquiry and purchase type thing, no different from the hundreds I had carried out to date. Except that this was reporting on my colleagues. Although I communicated with the shop staff from time to time when they helped me with news and profiles for my newsletter, I never had cause to visit any of the branches myself. It was unlikely the store staff would recognise me but there was a chance.

If I was recognised, it would put a whole new angle on the interaction – hopefully they would automatically be nicer but not necessarily – and could potentially put the whole programme in jeopardy, or at least my part in it. Although I had done much more complicated assignments with far more details to remember, these trips had an added frisson. I didn't want to be the company spy but, I convinced myself, it was for the benefit of the company's customer service. I briefly considered wearing glasses and putting on an accent for the duration of the visits.

Over a period of two months I travelled by train to Cardiff, Manchester, Bristol and Birmingham where I visited each Thomas Pink undercover as a customer needing help choosing a shirt for a male relative. I then made a purchase and hopped back on the train arriving back into central London right in the middle of rush hour. There certainly wasn't any time for shopping on company time. It was fun and it got me out of the office, out of London, and introduced me to towns I might never have otherwise seen. But it was lonely work. There were moments on the train where I sat, exhausted, thinking how much easier it would be to have just one job rather than always have to be rushing from one place to the other.

If TK Maxx is where fashion goes to die, then eBay, the world's largest global marketplace, is where it is resurrected. Created by Pierre Omidyar in 1995, the site was initially called AuctionWeb and sprang to life in Omidyar's San Jose living room, when he listed his broken laser pointer for sale and it eventually sold for $14. In 1997 he changed the name to eBay and in 2002 the company bought PayPal to run in conjunction with eBay. Millions of items are bought and sold daily, from jet planes to comics, with the occasional errant boyfriend thrown in for good measure. I am told there is even a market for used tights. It takes all sorts and if ever the saying that one man's trash is another man's treasure is appropriate, it is on eBay.

As with TK Maxx and the designer outlets, if you have a good eye you can pick up all sorts of amazing finds for next to nothing. Sadly, the days of making a fortune from your old cast-offs are over, but that doesn't mean you can't earn a decent bit of pocket money if you are prepared to put the time and effort into listing it all. I have financed holidays on the back of selling my stuff on eBay but it takes time. It's great that if you make a horrible mistake in TK Maxx or changed your mind about something that seemed a good idea when you took yourself shopping with raging PMT, there is always eBay to recoup your losses if you've left it too late for a refund.

What eBay and TK Maxx have in common is that they are like giant marketplaces where unearthing the good stuff requires a lot of stamina and a bit of nous. If only TK Maxx also had a search button.

CHAPTER EIGHT

The Isabel Marant for H&M Dress

I t's not just the retail industry that tempts us on a daily basis with what's new and must-have or 'limited edition'. The celebrity culture that feeds publications such as *heat*, *Grazia* and the *Daily Mail* is itself inextricably linked to fashion. If David and Victoria Beckham set the bar high by merging the multi-million pound worlds of football, pop and fashion, then those who follow them have their work cut out to emulate their idols. It was only a matter of time before celebrities started putting their names to clothing lines. By collaborating with high-street brands there was the potential to reach an even larger audience, enabling high-street consumers to buy into the designer lifestyles of the rich and famous. Suddenly a fragrance by Britney Spears that you could buy in Boots or Superdrug wasn't enough, shoppers wanted to be in David Beckham's pants, Kelly Brook's bikini and Rihanna's T-shirt.

Signing a celebrity who is associated with fashion by virtue of their style rather than their job is one thing, but signing the ultimate style icon, whose image and name had come to symbolise high-end brands the world over, was the biggest coup of all. Top Shop CEO Sir Philip Green was already a close friend of model Kate Moss – she allegedly refers to him as 'Uncle Phil' – so persuading her to design her own collection for Top Shop couldn't have been difficult. Either way, it was the collaboration to end all collaborations.

When in 2007 Moss launched her first range by posing as a live mannequin in the window of Top Shop in Oxford Circus, her supermodel tag was assured for another decade. At five floors and 95,000 square foot of selling space, Top Shop was the perfect space for the country's most successful model, in more ways than one. She was by now well into her thirties and a rare sight on the catwalks at fashion week, and yet she was still drawing fans from every age group. Most of the pieces from her collection, inspired by Moss's own favourite bits from her wardrobe, sold out immediately. Everyone from school-girls to fellow celebrities were able to own the laid-back rock-chic look epitomised by the publicity-shy model. Fourteen collections and a handful of tabloid-friendly 'drunken incidents' later, the Moss effect doesn't show any signs of slowing down.

The designer collaboration was kick started by the Designers at Debenhams range in 1993, to pull the department store chain out of the slump that hit it in the late eighties. Since then it's become a regular feature on the high street with three out of four customers citing it as their reason for shopping at Debenhams, according to marketing director Richard Cristofoli. Indeed, one pound out of every five spent in Debenhams is in this area. This enormously successful formula has gone from strength to strength. 'The design teams scour the up and coming shows at fashion week and sign up a rotating door of fresh talent which keeps the offering exciting and relevant,' says Richard.

H&M has this down to a fine art, with each collaboration gaining more momentum than the last. Starting with a collection designed by Karl Lagerfeld in 2004, the Swedish brand, led by CEO Karl-Johan Persson, has negotiated collaborations with Stella McCartney, Lanvin, Versace, Jimmy Choo, Isabel Marant, Alexander Wang and most recently Balmain. The collaborations have helped to increase awareness of H&M worldwide and according to Ann-Sofie Johansson, head of design for new development, who started there as a salesgirl, there is no reason not to continue with more in the future.

The more exclusive the designer involved, the more the consumers went mad for it, queuing up outside the flagship store in London's Oxford Street from the early hours and grabbing whatever they could in the strict time slot allotted to them. Experience has taught the brand to put a limit of one item per size per customer but still the most coveted pieces appear on eBay within hours of the doors opening. The H&M website invariably crashes before the 9 a.m. online start time, and if you do choose your items and reach the checkout page, you are unfailingly informed the items have already sold out.

When one of the most anticipated collections to date was launched, my friend Sophie and I were at our laptops, garments chosen, credit cards at the ready. Isabel Marant for H&M had been announced several months before, had been previewed by *Grazia* and trending on Twitter, so it was always going to be a bun fight. The website crashed and panic set in. And then Sophie, who is never knowingly fobbed off, had the innovative idea to use the telephone, the good old landline no less! After several minutes on hold, I got through to an actual living and breathing person, who was able to kindly inform me that the suede slouchy boots I had set my heart on were already sold out in my size. I plumped for a dress instead, because you absolutely can't go through all that only to come away with nothing. They're not stupid these people at H&M. The aforementioned dress, some two years later, is still to be found on eBay for twice its original £69.99 RRP.

*

It's a rare thing in this age of discounts and vouchers to pay more for clothing rather than less. In the noughties it seemed possible to avoid paying full price for anything. Promotional evenings, discounts and multi-buy offers were there at the drop of a Google search, and money-off vouchers courtesy of magazines and networking forums were never very far away. When the recession hit, not only were there the inevitable store closures that resulted in fewer mystery-shopping assignments, but customer service took a back seat in many stores as retailers relied more heavily on discounts and incentives to lure customers back.

Loyalty cards, or reward cards as they are sometimes known, appeared on the scene in 1982 when Homebase launched its Spend and Save card. However, loyalty programmes had actually been in existence in some form far longer. It was a great treat in our household to be given the Co-op's Green Shield stamp book to fill in on a rainy afternoon. And remember taking lemonade bottles back to the shop? Nowadays the bottles are plastic and children aren't allowed anywhere near fizzy drinks, but back in the day, Dad used to buy armfuls of the stuff. Luckily for us kids, our parents were strict about teeth brushing, otherwise the three of us would probably be toothless by now.

Interestingly, the loyalty card market in the UK is the most significant in the world, and there are now very few chains that don't run some sort of programme. In

1997 Boots launched its loyalty scheme, which is now the biggest worldwide with over 16 million people holding cards. It is also one of the most generous, with four points awarded for every pound. On my fortieth birthday I was able to buy every single product recommended (approximately £100 worth) during a Chanel makeover with my Boots points. Since then I've pocketed an electric toothbrush and a decent hairdryer.

In recording customer details, the retailer is then able to process their buying habits and make future offers accordingly. You are unlikely as a mum buying nappies and formula to be given a money-off voucher for men's deodorant, but an incentive to get an extra 100 points next time you spend over £40 might appeal.

The loyalty card is increasingly run alongside an app or mobile rewards program. Starbucks and Gourmet Burger Kitchen are front runners in this area with freebies dished out on a pleasingly regular basis. When my birthday comes round I find my inbox inundated with everything from offers of free bottles of prosecco in Pizza Express to a complimentary cookie at Subway. It all amounts to the same thing: lure the customer back in and then once you have them in your clutches upsell, upsell, upsell.

Turns out there are people who value their privacy over free stuff. Go figure. I was once standing in a queue at the checkout in Sainsbury's behind a well-dressed older gentleman who when asked for his Nectar card laughed ostentatiously and said, 'Let Sainsbury's know exactly what I'm buying so they can bombard me with offers and use all my details for market research? Not likely!' and off he went chortling and shaking his head with a knowing backwards glance to me, the gullible blonde waiting patiently to compromise my privacy with my Nectar card and money-off vouchers.

The lovely ladies who wax my legs at the frighteningly efficient Bare beauty salon in Battersea tell me that their concept is to be fast, friendly and reasonably priced. They also made the decision not to bother their customers with forms to fill in. Their regular clients come because they know they can nearly always fit in a last-minute appointment and the therapists don't object to babes in arms or toddlers having tantrums, so they can do without loyalty cards. However, they have found there are loyal and regular clients who actually *want* the company to have all their details. These customers are used to handing over their particulars and find it odd, frustrating even, that Bare don't have their details on file when they call in. Welcome to the world of yummy mummies who don't even have the time to give you their telephone number over the telephone.

Bare's owner and manager, Isabelle, who has run her business for ten years, laughs it off. She has a toddler and a new baby herself and being a beauty therapist, has seen and heard it all – they're not called therapists for nothing. You won't get offered a glass of chilled prosecco and a loyalty card at Bare, but you will get the fastest cleanest bikini wax in south-west London, and if your child doesn't get a school place or you've been threatened with redundancy, you will get a sympathetic ear and a shoulder to cry on too (so I've found).

At many retail outlets, management are keen to know from the mystery shopper that offers are being promoted by the staff. If a customer is buying items that can be bought on a 'buy three-for-two' deal, their attention should be drawn to the saving. Equally, asking about a loyalty card during the transaction is vital.

I have reported many times on one particular fast-food brand where unusually the operation isn't completely covert. If you have received exemplary service from someone who has gone the extra mile, then the staff member gets instantly rewarded. Out comes the congratulatory print out certificate with the promise of a £25 bonus for the staff member. Yes, it can be skin-crawlingly embarrassing.

I have felt terrible shyness on occasion and, although I am much better now, there have been times when I have frozen to the spot, unable to go through with a social situation with people I don't know. I still have moments when I can't face the task ahead. It's not uncommon for actors who feel quite at home onstage or in front of a camera to feel ill at ease when faced with being themselves in public. Mystery shopping is similar in that you're acting a part rather than being yourself and so embarrassment isn't such an issue.

On their job boards, mystery-shopping companies ask shoppers to read the brief through carefully to ensure they are completely comfortable with what is being asked of them before accepting an assignment.

There are several high-street fashion brands where the enjoyable stage of the assignment involves asking advice about a specific outfit, being guided by the assistant, trying things on and then buying something you've been recommended. I have been known to spend way longer in the fitting room than is required simply because I lose track of time being handed more and more lovely things to try. I genuinely enjoy this and have learnt a lot from seeing how different styles and cuts can flatter, enhance and disguise.

However, very few people enjoy the process of asking for a refund and I am no different in this respect. When the refund is less than half an hour later and is processed by the same staff member who has previously bust a gut to help you, it can feel rather mean. For me, it's awkward for everyone involved if I've been told to reveal that I'm a mystery shopper and the staff member wants to know how they've scored, sometimes even continuing to try to impress me. I'm not the sort of person who relishes that sort of power; I'm out of there as fast as possible.

I've always struggled with technology, but I was hearing whispers of this thing called Facebook and my sister urged me to take a look. That was how I found myself back in contact with Dan, the actor I met while filming in the Caribbean back in 1997. Our paths had crossed a couple of times in the way that actors' paths do – I'd seen him in things and we'd said hello. Communicating on Facebook was an excellent distraction. Dan quickly responded to my jokey message about our pretend marriage on the beach all those years ago. Now in his forties, Dan worked frequently, far more so than me, and had recently filmed a part in a BBC Jane Austen adaptation. As for me, at a bit of a crossroads and playing about with the idea of leaving acting for good, but it was fun to reminisce about the fun-filled sun-drenched job in the Caribbean.

I had finally moved on from my last disastrous relationship, so I was feeling very free and strangely hopeful. It was for this reason I allowed my sister to sign me up to the dating website MySingleFriend.com. I couldn't think of anything worse than going on a blind date, much less one conceived online, but I was persuaded by the possibility of material for my blog and it was summer, so I agreed to give it a go.

Everything I feared about this suddenly very popular way of dating came to fruition. Despite a glowing profile written by sister and friend Clare (both of them married with children themselves) and a not too shoddy photograph alongside, I failed to attract much interest and the little attention I did get didn't appeal to me. I am picky, I admit, but who isn't? I had two dates in total. One date could hardly hide his disappointment in me from the get-go while the other was lovely but we discovered three people we had in common – my sister Hannah, a colleague at Thomas Pink and an ex-boyfriend – all in the time it took me to drink one glass of wine. London is a huge city in a small dating world, it would seem. It just wasn't me either.

But it didn't seem such a leap of faith to meet up for a drink with Dan after numerous flirtatious emails and text conversations. I'm good at that kind of quick-fire wise-cracking on text and so was he, so I looked forward to the real thing. It seemed like it might be fun yet safe, and he was someone I already knew so it felt all right, that is to say, more all right than an Internet date.

We made a convincing and sweet couple in our roles in the Caribbean but that was down to Kerry's clever casting. We hadn't really clicked and, now, taking the sun, cocktails and wedding outfits out of the equation didn't help. We should have been older and wiser and yet it was almost bizarre how little either of us had changed. Him still prone to introspection; me just as likely to take the piss out of it.

Kerry herself was fairly nonplussed when I told her I'd been seeing Dan. She laughed and looked exasperated and I think said something along the lines of, 'Bloody actors . . .' She knew me well by this time and, as hook ups go, she couldn't see it working. Kerry was right, annoyingly she usually is.

The thing with Dan fizzled out after four months and I felt relieved that I'd come out of this one unscathed. I did what I always did: packed my diary full of jobs, went shopping, and talked my mum, brother and Rich into a weekend in Milan to see David Beckham play.

My brother had started working for an Internet start-up channel called ChannelBee, the brainchild of presenter Tim Lovejoy and financed by 19 Entertainment's Simon Fuller, former manager of the Spice Girls. The 19 offices were just down the road from the Thomas Pink head office where I worked, so it was easy to stop by in my lunch hour to record voiceovers when they needed a female voice. The other aspect about ChannelBee was the live webcam they had set up in their office. Channel 4's *Big Brother* was a big talking point by this time but webcams in offices? That was entirely new and as this particular office was full of faces recognisable from Sky One's popular Saturday morning show *Soccer AM*, it attracted a lot of attention to the ChannelBee website.

Following our return from Milan on the Monday morning, I got a call at work from my brother telling me to tune in to the webcam as they were about to have a visitor. I made myself a cup of tea and went into the IT department so we could all watch the events down the road unfold. The webcam flickered into focus to reveal Christophe standing with his ChannelBee compatriots, five thirty-something men standing in a row, all looking uncomfortable and not knowing what to do with their hands.

Suddenly, from the right of the screen, Tim Lovejoy appeared and he had someone with him. Fresh from his 5–0 win for AC Milan at the San Siro the night before, in walks David Beckham. The IT department and I watched in silence as the row of shuffling men at ChannelBee all stood up a little straighter and my brother Christophe shook Beckham's hand congratulating him on his performance. It might as well have been a royal visit and there was almost as much excitement down the road in the Thomas Pink offices. Not much work was done in Battersea that morning.

The ChannelBee team produced some truly brilliant work but sadly it was not meant to be. It was ahead of its time, webcam and all. Funds and morale were draining away and in 2010 it folded. I felt sad that my little brother wouldn't be working down the road from me any more.

However, as the year drew to a close it became clear that I probably wouldn't be working there for much longer either. I had discovered I was pregnant. On my own and between careers, it wasn't ideal. But you can wait a long time for ideal conditions, too long sometimes. I was more excited than I had ever been in my whole life, the time felt right and I could find no reason why not. Things were going to be rather different come the summer of 2010 and I couldn't have been happier about it.

CHAPTER NINE

A Pale-Blue Romper Suit and Matching Hat

There were some interesting discussions to get through first. Dan was understandably in turmoil, but this couldn't dampen my excitement. I enjoyed having this incredible secret and told no one but Dan, my mum, sister and Rich until well after the first twelve weeks. I wanted to be able to tell my closest friends in person, so I could see their faces and answer any questions they might have about how I would cope as a single mother. I have a wonderful bunch of friends but nevertheless I was surprised when without exception every single one of them reacted with joy, excitement and positivity. Those who were mothers themselves were thrilled and assured me it would be the best thing I ever did, which only added to my excitement.

My friend Clare was also pregnant with her second child, and so the timing was perfect as far as she was concerned. We giggled like teenagers as we compared gory pregnancy details and possible names. She wanted me to have a girl as she already had one herself and felt the shopping opportunities would be better. I didn't want to find out, relishing the thought of the surprise at the end of it all.

Clare looked huge, with a bump that seemed to appear overnight, while mine took ages to come out. That stage where you look to anyone else as if you may have merely overindulged at lunch is frustrating. The two of us visited maternity shops on a mission to find Clare a dress to wear to her mother-in-law's wedding, and as Clare tried on pretty frocks, I was outside the fitting room dropping into conversation with the shop staff that I too was pregnant. I looked forward to the new challenge of pregnancy dressing when the annoying nausea had passed and my Top Shop jeans would no longer do up.

One morning I stood in front of a mirror at home and marvelled at my slightly bloated tummy. This could be it, I thought, I may never have a flat stomach again. To my surprise the thought made me smile. Having fretted about my curves and the squidgy parts of my anatomy, I now couldn't care less how they ended up. My body felt comfortable in its present state, almost as if it was relieved to be put to good use.

Maternity wear is another part of the clothing industry that has had new life breathed into it. In fact, a whole industry devoted to it had blossomed since the seventies when I was born. My mum made her own maternity dresses when she was pregnant, they were tent-like and well, mumsy, and there wasn't a Lycra-wrapped stomach in sight. When, to my horror, my already ample bosom expanded three sizes, I spent hours browsing online for nursing bras, the cup of which would have comfortably encased my considerably sized head. For the rest of me, I invested wisely in 'skinny' (oh the irony) maternity jeans from Gap but shopped at Primark for non-maternity stretchy dresses in larger sizes that cost next to nothing.

That was how I ended up being dressed head to toe in Primark upon meeting Sarah Jessica Parker and the rest of the *Sex and the City* crowd. The shame of it! My sister Hannah, who now had her own showbiz show called *Spotlight* at Sky News Active, was interviewing the whole cast who were over for the release of the second *Sex and the City* film and she invited me along to Claridge's to sit in. Had I been my usual shape rather than seven months pregnant, I would have spent so long agonising over what to wear in front of Sarah Jessica Parker that I would probably never have made it on time. As it was, it was hot and sticky and I was hotter and stickier than most, so I threw on a nautical-looking £8 Primark dress with a pair of ballet pumps and ran to the station to meet Hannah for a debriefing.

The four actresses were lovely and every bit as glamorous as you would hope, SJP tiny and sparkly eyed in a green number that lit up her face and Kristin Davis, who played Charlotte York, smiley and giggly in elegant cream. Mr Big actor, Chris Noth, admitted to taking Big's designer suits home from the set. With the exception of Kim Cattrall, who was much gentler than her character Samantha, the *Sex and the City* girls seemed remarkably similar to their onscreen personas, but I shouldn't have been surprised. Rarely is casting noticeably far-fetched, not unless you find yourself in 'character' role territory.

As one by one these familiar faces sat down in front of Hannah like old pals, all I could do was sit there trying not to sweat in my state of advanced pregnancy.

'Are you okay?' Sarah Jessica Parker asked me, a kind look of concern etched on her immaculately made-up face, all green sparkle and fluttery eyelashes.

'Oh yes, I'm fine, just a bit warm, I had to run, well hurry, to get here on time,' I stuttered.

'Do you need a glass of water?'

Oh god this was embarrassing, let's talk about you, SJP, not me! Hannah must be cursing me. I hoped this wasn't being timed as part of the precious five minutes she'd been allocated by the *Sex and the City* PR.

'No, no, honestly I'm fine, I have some water in my

bag, I'm sorry my shoes are so awful . . .' There it was, I'd given Sarah Jessica no choice other than to look at my pink Primark pumps.

Sarah Jessica looked at my pink Primark pumps.

'Oh they're cuuute!' exclaimed the lovely SJP as she leant around Hannah to get a better view of my feet. I explained to the sympathetic SJP that I was running around town all day and it simply wasn't practical getting on and off tubes but how mortified I was nevertheless.

'Why didn't you put your heels in your purse?' she asked quizzically. 'You could have swapped them over once you were in here sitting down and then changed back into the little cute shoes afterwards.'

As I said, SJP was sympathetic, but she wasn't going to let me get away with it. A lady after my own heart. I had let myself down sartorially speaking and I was cross with myself. It was a momentary lapse of concentration, I decided, blame it on baby brain, that seemed to be the thing to say, although I didn't buy it myself.

In 2010 the pressure was on to look fabulous all through pregnancy, immediately after pregnancy and for offspring to be as complementary as a Hermès handbag. Even if you successfully negotiate pregnancy in your late thirties, avoid stretch marks and go back to work in your size 10 jeans, you still feel the need to look like you are in your late twenties with a little help from a syringe full of god knows what. The bar has been raised and there is no telling how much further it will go.

Thank goodness for Top Shop, ASOS and H&M, whose maternity collections means the nine months of pregnancy wasn't quite the style wilderness it once was. Some of us felt terrific while growing a small human being in our tummies and wanted to look terrific too. If you did feel inclined to spend a little more on your bump wardrobe, then Serafina and Isabelle Olivier were sophisticated bets for those who neither wanted to look like Kim Kardashian nor wanted to appear as if they have cut a head-sized hole in a marquee and stuck their head through it. It didn't occur to me at the time that it was worth spending a little more on attractive maternity clothes that fit well, so thoroughly was I embracing not having a waistline to worry about.

I lost count of the number of times I was told that eventually I would lose my appetite as the baby grew bigger and took up the space where my bottomless pit of a stomach used to be. Indeed, I had witnessed my sister pick at little morsels of food towards the end of both her pregnancies and I dreaded the thought of it. Where's the fun in that? I didn't mind not drinking for nine months but not being able to eat a whole pizza? No, that didn't sit well with me at all.

I was an exception to the rule as it happened. As my due date approached, I was still eating full meals, still wearing heels and still out most nights of the week.

Hannah passed all her baby stuff onto me and so the only thing I had to shop for was a pram. My mum took me to John Lewis where I balked at the cost and scoffed at the suggestion that I might need such a thing as a cup holder. I didn't have to make any plans at all, which meant I wasn't really mentally prepared for the event that was about to happen. The minute the midwife who took the antenatal class I attended announced 'Babies can't read birthing plans, so you might as well tear yours up right now!' I switched off. I read a few books I was given ('How to dress like a Rock Star Mom' was particularly informative) but as soon as I got to a bit about supportive birthing partners having 'Go Mommy!' or 'Team Emily!' T-shirts printed up for the delivery room, I decided my time was better spent elsewhere and went back to my *Grazia*.

But after nine months of window shopping and imagining a day when I might be able to see my legs, let alone fit them into my old jeans, the summer fashion on *Grazia*'s pages were beginning to do my head in. Eventually I stopped looking and focused my attention on baby stuff, which I realised I hadn't done before for fear of tempting fate.

With a website now being a prerequisite for any business or service, many brands in the retail industry were finding their website was their most lucrative 'branch'. In the early noughties huge international companies such as Chanel, H&M and Zara had websites that were merely showrooms for their collections with no means of being able to shop from them. The sites looked great but the intricate logistics of browsing, selecting, purchasing, shipping and then potentially returning goods was very much in its infancy and where sites like AsSeenOnScreen.com (now ASOS), net-a-porter.com and Figleaves.com led, riding the wave to enormous success, not all others who followed had such a smooth ride.

Sean Farrell was a director at Office London when the first Office website launched and was instrumental in its conception. Having managed the original mail-order department that went on to become office.co.uk, Sean then oversaw the design of the second website, a more advanced and modern version compared to the nineties original. The Internet was a new tool for the retail industry, there was a lot of trial and error. Sean remembers:

'We didn't have a clue. If there were any consultants in those days, we didn't use one. What I quickly learnt, however, was the more stores we opened, the busier our website became.'

Nicola Bryan-Jones is an area manager for Japanese high-street interiors store Muji and started her career on the shop floor at Thomas Pink. She agrees with Sean when she says that stores tend to work well as a showcase for products, especially investment pieces. The Muji consumer in particular likes to feel the product, try it, see the colour – furniture can be tried out in the first instance but then often it turns out to be easier to order it online.

'I think consumers are a lot more choosy now and [at Muji] it works vice versa with consumers doing their research online and then going into the store knowing exactly what they want.' Nicola says. At Muji their mystery shoppers' feedback is given straight to the branch managers. The results are then used for training exercises.

Nicola was promoted from the shop floor at Thomas Pink into retail operations, eventually area managing several high-street branches. She has seen a lot of change on the high street during her career but how much more change can the British high street take I wonder?

'At the moment I think the Internet and the high street work hand in hand but I imagine as technology grows it will become easier to have an all-round experience online,' Nicola muses, before adding, 'We've already seen [in a relatively short space of time] how delivery times have been cut to a few hours, some online retailers have made it a very efficient process indeed!'

Debenhams' Richard Cristofoli pinpoints speed and convenience of delivery as a priority. 'In Christmas 2013 convenience overtook price. It wasn't good for us because our multi-channel delivery proposition was two or three years behind – we couldn't offer next day delivery or click and collect,' he says. 'Within twelve months we addressed that and now you can get next-day delivery if you order by midnight or next-day click and collect if you order by 9 p.m.'

Fashion websites need to look eye-catching, with garments showed off in their best light and with as many angles and zoom-in shots as possible, but it is the technology that is separating the wheat from the chaff. A relatively new feature, the moving catwalk image, is still not widely available (ASOS, Oasis and Thomas Pink are high-street brands with this option) while the virtual fitting room is even rarer.

Every single product needs to be represented with as much detail both pictorially and with the written descriptions alongside because it's not just shifting the stock off the warehouse shelves at full price that is the target, but ensuring it doesn't get sent back for a refund. Offers of free delivery and returns are enticing but the last thing the retailer wants is for the extra sales to come straight back. Where previously this was a huge issue for retailers, improved and more informative websites together with better customer service involving real people rather than an automated telephone service, have reduced returns in recent years. The forecast is positive for online retailers with 40% of all retail sales being attributed to online sales by 2020 and customer returns down to 10%. However, there is still a long way to go in this area according to Sean Farrell who claims, 'Online returns are a nightmare from the retailers' perspective, full stop. That hasn't changed from what I can tell.'

Whenever there is a surge in sales, inevitably there will be a surge in returns, I witnessed this first hand at Thomas Pink after each Christmas period and after a sale. The mind boggles to think how the larger retailers cope after Black Monday and worse, Cyber Monday.

Pascale de l'Eprevier started her childrenswear website Orfeo in 2007 and agrees that in her experience the returns rate has actually increased since she launched her company. 'I think people were more afraid of returning things in the early days,' she says. 'But in recent years the rate has been stable. I have a lot of orders from the U.S. and Asia and that helps keep it down as it's expensive for those overseas customers to return goods.'

Not surprisingly it is the Internet-based retailers who are the front runners in this area. With huge amounts of stock updated daily, blogs, 'web exclusives' and personal stylists available for live web chats, even same day delivery in a few cases, no wonder the high street is struggling to compete.

Pascale knows only too well the pros and cons of an Internet-based start-up business and she is the first to admit that she had absolutely no experience in building a website business before she launched her own site. What she did have was experience in marketing, finance and strategy from her formative years working for large corporations.

'That helped a lot,' admits Pascale.

My baby was born a week late on 11 August 2010: eight pounds six ounces and fifty-two centimetres of pure joy. He was too long to fit into the baby boy Babygro I had, so he spent his first day on earth in a pink one which had belonged to my niece Phoebe. I was ecstatic.

While Dan and I were sometimes at loggerheads due to a totally different outlook on parenting, we were utterly united in our delight and love for this perfect little boy. Jake, as we eventually agreed to name him, appeared with very little warning courtesy of an impromptu C-section performed in a side room, actually little more than a cupboard, at Kingston hospital, with my mum thankfully arriving just in time to scrub in and watch over the whole event. I had gone to the hospital for a check-up after tea and a natter with my friend Rich. I texted Dan and my mum to say I was fine and would be back in time for dinner but I wasn't. I didn't even have my carefully prepared overnight bag with me – my brother had to bring it up to the hospital later that night so that both baby and I had some clothes. Yet another occasion when I wasn't dressed as I'd like to have been.

It still makes me smile when I think about the role Facebook played in my life – had it not existed, I would quite probably not have had Jake and that makes it a pretty amazing thing. Anything that encourages communication has to be a good thing, right?

It sounds obvious now, but Jake's arrival provided an immediate common ground for Dan and me that I hadn't dared to hope for while I was pregnant. When Dan wasn't working he was around to help, and the three of us spent a great deal of time together. Jake was an almost unnervingly good sleeper and so we had a lot of fun.

*

My brother and his girlfriend Lucy made the decision to have their wedding on 2 October 2010. This was eight weeks after my due date, so I immediately went into a panic about what I would wear and how it would be almost impossible to shop for an outfit until the day was almost upon us.

My mum had slightly more practical concerns: 'Can you not make it a bit later? What if Emily's overdue? It's bound to be late, she's always late . . .'

Radio silence from my brother.

'Oh god, what if she has to have a Caesarean? What if the baby's late *and* she has to have surgery?'

But the date was set in stone. August arrived.

The baby was late and I had to have surgery.

My sister Hannah and I organised a trip to Bicester Village with our small boys three weeks before the wedding. Hannah was now working for Sky part-time after having her two children and I was on maternity leave, so we plotted to go on a Monday morning when we might have more chance of moving freely with our two prams. Both of us needed to find something to wear for Christophe's wedding and this seemed like a good opportunity to make a day of it. We bundled my two-and-a-half-year-old nephew and newborn son into Hannah's car, full of excitement about our adventure.

My excitement was short-lived. It became clear that

while the lower half of my body had miraculously gone back to its former shape and I had no discernible tummy at all, my top half was still untenably huge. The boobs which had seemed to grow the minute I conceived were doing the job for which they were intended admirably, but it was almost impossible to find anything to fit them into.

My endlessly hungry baby cried in his pram as we wandered around the shops while my nephew Curtis behaved like an angel, laughing at anything and everything. I very quickly lost my sense of humour. What had started out as fun descended into misery for me as dress after dress had to be rejected. My lovely lean sister, meanwhile, was spoilt for choice and looked amazing in everything she put on. I could feel the ugly green monster rising in me. Hannah being Hannah spotted the signs and suggested we break for lunch.

As we sat in Starbucks feeding our starving children, I stared blackly into the middle of the table, wondering what I was going to do.

'It would be easier if I was huge all over rather than this grotesque top-heavy version of myself I've become,' I muttered, trying not to sob. If I started I wouldn't stop, I was only four weeks into motherhood after all.

I could see Hannah desperately trying to smother laughter at my melodramatic use of the word 'grotesque'.

'There isn't much here, is there, it's a bit crap. Perhaps we should have gone to Westfield instead . . .' she gently suggested.

'It isn't crap, it's me, I'm crap! You're fine, you could wear anything and look amazing, I'm going to look like a giant inflatable version of Dolly Parton no matter what I wear and you'll look thin and gorgeous.' There it was, my sense of humour had well and truly left the building. I was making a scene.

Hannah finally gave way to laughter in the middle of a mouthful of ham and cheese toastie, which flew out across the table at me. 'How is an inflatable version of Dolly Parton worse off than actual Dolly Parton?' she choked and spluttered.

'Because an inflatable Dolly Parton can't even sing "Islands in the Stream", that's why,' I shot back.

'Fair point,' said Hannah, who had done a very good job of diffusing the situation by almost choking to death.

'And you're married!' I added as an afterthought, though even I knew that was a long shot.

'What?' said Hannah turning to wipe Curtis's face with the soggy napkin.

'No one's going to be looking at you thinking, look at the state of her, no wonder she's not married.'

I was beginning to wish I could rewind the whole conversation.

'No, they're all going to be looking at Lucy and Christophe instead. Now let's go and get the babies some stuff in White Company and then go home.'

As I sat in the car on the way home from Bicester I realised that the answer was to find myself a skirt and top in different sizes rather than a dress which was either going to be too small on the top or way too big on the bottom. I didn't want to emphasise the size of my chest, but it would make me feel better to be able to show off the slim bits on the bottom, so I would have to focus on colour as well as fabric. Not only did I need an open neckline to avoid looking like I'd stuffed two balloons down my top, but logistically it would help to have 'easy access' – I didn't want to spend half of my brother's wedding reception shut away breast-feeding in the loos. A light and drapey fabric like silk would be best (although god forbid any leakages) and preferably in a darker colour to play down the curves. On the bottom, I would wear something fitted and structured to show off the slim part.

Statement accessories are a good way of drawing attention away from those areas on which you are less keen, and I decided you don't get much more distracting than a newborn baby. But never had amazing shoes seemed so important. My baby hadn't arrived as predicted on 4 August but my heavily reduced D&G suede stilettos from BrandAlley did! Sometimes you just have to plan an outfit from the feet up.

At the next opportunity a few days later my mum took charge of Jake and sent me out into Kingston town centre on a mission. I had checked out the Coast website and earmarked a delicate silk blouse that looked roomy, so I headed straight to Coast, picked out the biggest size they had and headed to the fitting room. Coast is generous in its sizing and the first top I tried was too big. Excellent, that was exactly what I'd hoped, a little boost to start off the proceedings. The size down was much better, and although the blouse was reminiscent of some sort of Victoriana nightwear you might wear with bloomers, with only a week to go until the wedding I didn't have a choice. The skirt part was simple. Coast had a lovely black lace pencil skirt that held me in and emphasised my returning waistline, so I'd feel good in that. Two days before the wedding, I had shrunk even further so I took the skirt back and exchanged it for a size 8.

By the time my eyelash extensions were in place (more distraction), I felt more or less like myself again. I wore the lacy Coast outfit just the once and soon after the wedding I sold it on eBay.

Jake wore a gorgeous pale-blue romper suit and matching hat, which Lucy had bought him. The outfit lasted until about halfway through the ceremony when he pooed all over it. As Lucy and Christophe walked back down the aisle as man and wife and their guests filed out of the church, I was on my knees in the vestibule, changing the sodden nappy, wiping poo off the floor tiles and stuffing soiled baby wipes into my clutch bag.

CHAPTER TEN

The McQ Tuxedo Jacket

ocation, location, location, as the saying goes. And that can mean anything from being at the right end of a very expensive and well-known street to being the first brand you encounter when turning left at the top of the escalator on the first floor of Dickens and Jones in Richmond, as Clare and I discovered all those years ago when the new Episode concession was launched there. Just as nobody wants to be positioned on the top floor in the corner right by the toilets, there's not much use being on Sloane Street if it's the bit without shops on.

Given that shop windows can make the difference between enticing a customer inside or not, it's not surprising that they're the first thing to come under scrutiny on a mystery-shopping report: if the customers aren't tempted to come in then the staff can't make the sales. Is the window attractive? Is it clean and well lit? Are the products priced clearly? Does the display make you want to go into the shop? The efforts of the company's visual display team are also monitored and the staff's knowledge of what is in the window and where to locate it is a question that comes up regularly on reports.

Visual display staff or 'window dressers', as they used to be known, are the unsung heroes of a brand. Regularly working unsociable hours so as not to disrupt the day-to-day business or leave the windows bare for too long, this team has to think about Christmas trees in August and is then inevitably working late into the night on Christmas Eve to prepare the shop for the start of the sale on Boxing Day. There is a lot of lugging boxes, ironing and pinning involved in the life of a visual display merchandiser.

Over the years the Christmas windows of London's main department stores have taken on a competitive element, with Liberty and Harvey Nichols battling against Selfridges and Harrods for the most memorable displays. My brother and I once appeared in a Thomas Pink window display in the lead up to Christmas. We made our way to Mary Portas's Yellow Door PR company off Tottenham Court Road where we posed for photographs in party hats pulling all manner of stupid faces. Print-outs of our faces were then cut out and stuck to mannequins wearing TP shirts and put in the festive windows of all the stores in the UK. Our parents were most amused, never more so than when they left for a holiday to Antigua and spotted us both airside in the branch at Heathrow airport.

The area just inside the shop entrance is one of the most important areas on the shop floor, setting the scene for the customer and hopefully luring them in further. Within the first minute, retailers try to gently coerce the customer into spending their money using sound, sight and smell, and sometimes even touch and taste. As a mystery shopper you are expected to notice and make a note of everything from the lighting (are any light bulbs out?) to the music, scent and any eye-catching promotions. The types and levels of all these elements are individual to each store depending on their demographic and branding.

Even the direction you walk around the shop in is dictated by the store designers. On entering a shop, the majority of shoppers will naturally look to the left before turning to the right and then working their way around the shop in an anti-clockwise direction. The layout of the product is designed to cash in on this with the newest, most eye-catching and often most expensive stock mer-chandised at the front, on the right-hand side. Don't expect any of the basics or staple pieces to be easy to find either – these everyday items which tend not to be the big money spinners will be right at the back of the store, forcing you to walk past everything else on offer. River Island always places their three-for-two plain T-shirts at the back of the store while H&M merchandise their fitness wear at the back, usually close to the fitting rooms.

Former head of store design at Thomas Pink, Kevin Knox, explains: 'A shop unit is divided into areas and the further back into the unit you go, the less the rent per square foot costs. So a wide shop front will cost a lot more than a narrow shop that goes far back, because there is more selling space on the shop floor at the front near the entrance.

'Brands will always place their most popular and successful pieces right at the front where customers will see them as soon as they arrive. This is the most expensive part of the shop in terms of rent and so they put their biggest sellers there.' Kevin illustrates this point with the department store layout: 'You will always find perfumes and cosmetics and small leather goods right by the entrance in a department store because these products are what they make the most money from. There's no point in having big expensive items that a store will only sell one of once in a while right out front, it's a waste of space.'

That is why, according to Kevin, it was crazy to put a cafe area right at the front of a unit, as was previously the case with the flagship DKNY in Bond Street in London. 'It's a great idea and it may lure people in, but after they've had their coffee and cake the potential customer might very well leave without even venturing into the shop. This space on one of London's premier shopping streets was costing a fortune and you simply can't earn the money back selling cakes and sandwiches.'

And what shopper isn't distracted in a long and boring queue for the till by the little stocking-filler bits of nonsense lining the route? Socks, sweets, bangles, iPhone cases, gloves and hair accessories are all impulse buys that earn their keep in the empty space filled up by waiting customers. 'At Office we always had the children's shoes by the counter, especially the toddler shoes because they prompted the "Ahh" reaction and that would turn into an impulse buy,' says former Office London director Sean Farrell. 'I defy any mum or auntie not [to want] to buy Baby Uggs on sight.'

Nothing is left to chance in a high-street store: the tempo and volume of the music playing will depend on the targeted customers – loud and upbeat for the young and fashionable to send the heartbeat racing (Hollister and Abercrombie & Fitch, for example), softer and more mellow for the more considered, older and potentially better-off customer (Massimo Dutti and Anthropologie). Generally speaking, slower music encourages the customer to linger. At the American brand Victoria's Secret, a brand aimed at the younger end of the shopper scale, there is soothing music played into their branches with the idea that it facilitates discussions with the sales assistants, in turn presenting the opportunity for an unpushy sales pitch.

The lower table displays of folded items or accessories often placed at the front of a store are so that the customer can see right through to the rest of the shop floor, while the flooring itself is carefully chosen according to area. A smooth floor guides the customer in while a carpeted floor will slow the customer down and encourage them to browse and look more closely.

And have you noticed how brands now tend to be recognisable by their scent? The evocative smell of baby powder, for example, is used by childrenswear shops to evoke a sense of security and nostalgia. It is widely accepted that a floral smell encourages shoppers to not only browse for longer but also to spend more. A mint aroma will make the customer more alert, compared to the relaxing scent of vanilla. A study by neurologist and psychiatrist Dr Alan Hirsch, who specialises in the treatment of smell and taste loss, found that 84 per cent of people were willing to pay $10 more for a pair of Nike shoes in a scented room versus those in an unscented room.

Hugo Boss uses the same scent – musk with a hint of citrus – in all its stores. Having recently undergone a £3-million refurbishment, the branch of Hugo Boss in London's Sloane Square now has a luxurious private shopping area in the basement where big-spenders are ushered to relax with a glass of champagne. Subliminal smells, alcohol and the collections brought to you as you put your feet up, how can it fail? Burberry too aims to get their repeat customers sitting down as quickly as possible.

Beware the mystery-shopping assignment carried out on an empty stomach. Having been encouraged to sit down with a glass of champagne in a high-profile footwear branch one lunchtime, I almost spent £500 on a pair of shoes myself. When I was being paid a mere £10 for the job, this was very nearly disastrous. I resisted, I'm happy to say, but left the shop and its expensive shoes feeling quids in and ready to spend money frivolously in Aldo instead.

The high-street favourite H&M has a distinctive smell that hits you before you've gone through the door, so if you're walking down Oxford Street engrossed in conversation with a friend, you will instantly know you are walking past an H&M, even with your head turned in the opposite direction. Indeed, the New York department store Bloomingdale's pumps out different scents in different rooms – coconut for the swimwear department, for example, and lilac in the lingerie department.

It's no coincidence that Hollister's dimly lit noisy nightclub atmosphere is accompanied by the strong sweet smell of their signature fragrances. Tester bottles are placed at the till to encourage the young clientele to spray it as they wait to pay. It also hasn't hurt having male-model types folding T-shirts either. My thirteen-year-old goddaughter Jess would shop in Hollister more if it was cheaper; her mum Clare says she wants a grey top with the Hollister branding and it's fifty pounds. Sixteen-year-old Ruby thinks the atmosphere is cool, if a bit dark and the male models are a plus. She says she and her friends are less interested in brands and it would be a sin to wear a T-shirt saying Hollister on it. My ever-youthful mum (a slim and spritely sixty-eight-year-old who cycles everywhere and still works as a nurse in the local surgery), goes into her local Hollister in Kingston-upon-Thames specifically to spritz herself with one of their own-brand fragrances whenever she's passing. In order to do this she has to walk past all of the new stock to reach the counter.

My niece Phoebe, my mum's one and only grand-daughter, is now eleven years old so Mum has the perfect excuse to frequent Hollister, but does she use it? No. My mum is the only person I know over the age of sixteen who regularly buys clothes for herself from there! It had been reported that direct spending by teenagers and children has tripled since 1990 with the finger pointed at popular culture, which is increasingly synonymous with fashion and advertising campaigns aimed at younger consumers. I wonder if the figures factor in sixty-eight-year-olds buying stuff for themselves.

Just as smell and sound are used to manipulate and cajole, so sight is used to full effect too with colour schemes chosen carefully to maximise sales. It is believed that navy attracts bargain hunters, blue is welcoming, green is unsurprisingly associated with nature and yellow with happiness. Red will evoke a sense of danger or, as the SALE signs in shop windows prove only too well, urgency. These colour schemes have been narrowed down to fit with two major shopping tribes – the impulse buyer (these are born, not made, like both my parents) who are attracted by warm colours and the buyer with a plan (oh, to be a shopper with a list I actually stick to) who favours the cooler shades.

There is less research into touch in terms of the retail experience, but it is something that is being exploited more and more. After all, it's not just curious toddlers who want to touch everything in shops. A pile of neatly folded cashmere jumpers is begging to be stroked in the same way that a small fluffy kitten is. You know how it should feel, but human beings are programmed to check it really does feel the way we think it should, just to be absolutely certain. Stores such as Primark, which prides itself on its no-frills style of interior décor, may even deliberately leave that messy pile of unpaired shoes and flip-flops on the floor. An immaculate rail of untouched garments may be pleasing to the eye of a visual display manager, but does it look so perfect that customers don't like to touch it?

'Displays need to be relevant to the audience,' says Melanie Traub. 'The customer wants to feel the full-price offer and the customer wants to feel this is special. The "stuck in" look works best for discounting.'

It's no wonder then that most of us often buy items of clothing that then sit unworn in the back of our wardrobes: we are being targeted by highly skilled and aggressive marketeers with decades of research into the public's shopping habits behind them.

On becoming a parent, you suddenly see shopping malls and department stores through different eyes. There are stairs or escalators to be negotiated, a lift somewhere if you can locate it, and delicate-looking displays to steer toddlers and prams away from. I don't have one of those big petrol-guzzling cars but I did have what seemed to me to be a ridiculously large and unwieldy pushchair in which to cart my very small son around in. I would struggle to get through shop doors with it, smash it into tables and other shoppers' legs once inside and then wonder what on earth to do with it when I wanted to try something on in a minuscule fitting-room cubicle.

I experimented with one of those Baby Bjorn things. It worked so well for Dan, who managed to look cool with Jake stuck to his front like some kind of statement necklace. However, Dan is six foot three. I am five foot five and Jake was fifty-two centimetres at birth. He got longer by the day so having Jake hang down my front meant his long flailing legs were constantly bouncing off my knees. It was a shame because those hooks in fitting rooms looked very tempting: if only I could have hooked Jake in his Baby Bjorn to the cubicle wall.

Once he was able to toddle about, Jake wanted to be out of the pram at every opportunity. If I kept him strapped in he would scream and kick and if I let him out he would disappear under a rail of hanging dresses within seconds. I'd find him sitting on the floor in the middle of a carousel of clothes, grinning and chewing on a plastic size-16 hanger tag. One day, I was adding up the items in my basket only vaguely aware of Jake's chattering, and the other customers in the queue were giggling and I wasn't sure why. I looked up to see Jake, who was listening attentively to the tannoy, repeating: 'Please go to cashmere number 5.' 'Please go to cashmere number 7.' It was then I decided perhaps he was spending too much time in shops.

I couldn't have predicted what good company my baby boy would be and I missed him dreadfully when I returned to work part-time at Thomas Pink, and when he was at his dad's every Sunday. Gut-wrenching just about sums it up. Jake, however, had a ball and through his weekly trips between north and south London, he developed an insatiable love of tall buildings. Jake became obsessed with the Shard after Dan took him to see it, which fortuitously we could see from St John's Hill in Clapham Junction. It seemed a good idea to feed this precocious fascination with architecture, so Jake and I visited Paris and Pisa.

When Jake spent time with his dad, I had time on my hands, even if it wasn't always welcome. One weekend, some old friends arranged an evening out in our old local haunt in Wimbledon. Over twenty years had gone by since the days of house parties and drinking cider on the common, and I felt a bit shy as I hadn't seen any of them in a while, but I braved it and went along to the pub on my own. Now I had Jake to talk about, a development this group perhaps hadn't seen coming, and as most of them now had children too it was good to be part of that exclusive club.

Gallons of water had passed under the bridge and yet looking around the table at everyone, these faces I knew so well, we could have been back in 1990. There were a few grey hairs but even the clothes didn't look that different. I was dressed all in black with a mannish-cut McQ jacket slung over the miniskirt and top I'd been wearing all day. In my rush to get out of the house, I hadn't made much effort. I'd been ill and was too thin, so for the first time in my life I wore clothes to try and bulk myself out. Other than that, things were very much the same.

At the end of the evening I was sweet-talked into giving four people a lift home, a journey that took me completely out of my way. Rupert, who had sat in his coat all evening, was the last to be dropped off. We were teenagers when we met, and both of us had been through a lot, but as we talked about our kids and work, the break-up of his marriage and the loss of my dad, I was surprised at how easy and comfortable it was. When I realised it was time to head home, I turned the key in the ignition but the battery was completely dead. Rupert ended up having to push the car to jump start it so I could get home.

Having devoted myself to my baby, it hadn't occurred to me to think about dating, but various friends had started to bug me about 'getting back out there' and not wanting to 'be alone for ever'. I was busy and Jake made me happier than I could have imagined. I loved our life together, and didn't want to complicate our situation. I wasn't negative about my prospects; I simply wasn't all that bothered about them. All the same, it was a pleasant surprise when Rupert rang me up, asking me out for a drink. I knew it couldn't hurt, it would be fun and I didn't have to worry about impressing him or any of that nonsense, he knew exactly what he was letting himself in for after all. I could afford to be laid back about it too, none of that panicking about what to wear malarkey. As if . . .

Removing all your clothes repeatedly can be demoralising and a right-old faff for even the most dedicated of shoppers; for others it simply isn't worth the hassle compared to trying a purchase on at home and then bringing it back if it's not right. Although fitting rooms are a hundred times better than they were in the seventies when they were mostly communal, many shoppers still avoid them.

Service at the fitting room is a vital part of the selling process for many higher-end brands and there is much attention to detail here in mystery-shopping reports. For example, where an alteration service is available, the staff member needs to be on hand to comment on the fit of an item, suggest an alternative size where necessary, fetch it and then introduce the alteration service and/or the refund policy where appropriate. Higher-end brands are hot on this aspect of their service and a quarter of a report can be devoted to it. Other questions on the form are: were the cubicles clean, pleasant-smelling and free from hangers? Did the assistant count the items in and count them out again? Did the assistant remain nearby and remove unwanted items? Did they introduce additional and complementary items?

For many, the idea of having any input at all from a member of staff who could after all be half your age is enough to put you off trying things on at all; for others it is a genuine help. The mark of a truly good shop assistant is when they not only suggest items you would never have considered yourself but then go on to convince you of its worth by demonstrating its versatility through different styling techniques. Ultimately you want to be shown you can look amazing without feeling that you have been pressured into buying things you don't need or want. Sales assistants who manage to help you without being pushy or overbearing are rare, but they do exist. I like to think that mystery shopping in its own little way is striving towards a high street where you can expect service to 'go the extra mile', but the reality is, more often than not, merely 'meeting your expectations'.

Nowadays, when I catch sight of myself in a shop window, I am shocked at how much older I look than I had imagined – it certainly never happens the other way around, more's the pity. We have complicated relationships with our bodies, and once your body has gone through pregnancy, childbirth and breast-feeding, you wonder if you will ever look at it in the same way again. Or more importantly, will anyone else?

Still, fitting rooms are improving all the time and gimmicks from lighting to tricksy mirrors are used to improve the experience. I love a mirror that makes me look as if I'm built like Elle McPherson as much as the next person, but I am amazed at how many women don't notice their elongated selves staring back at them in some of the most popular shops. I have taken pictures of myself in what I believe to be super-flattering mirrors in Zara, H&M and Gap so I have photographic evidence of long legs I absolutely do not possess. It's body dysmorphia in reverse.

So if the high street now has the distorted mirrors, what are the really flashy places doing? Well, the new Harvey Nichols in Birmingham boasts 360-degree 'delay' mirrors with in-built video camera. Exclusive to their 'style-concierge' lounge, these mirrors enable VIP customers to set the in-built camera to film themselves doing their very own 'Zoolander' routine, play it back to themselves to assess how they look and then share the footage on Twitter, Facebook or wherever. Is this facility not begging to have endless imaginary Oscar acceptance speeches filmed on it? Or Bananarama dance routines? My friend Rich would be all over a cover of Take That's

'Pray' while for me, it'd be my award-winning Vogueing at Set nightclub in Faliraki (circa August 1990).

In America, interactive mirrors by Panasonic that suggest suitable products for just about every inch of your face and body are being trialled. No more worrying about the sales assistant barging in when you're starkers then. How useful that interactive mirror would have been in the lead up to my date!

While in my twenties the default evening outfit was jeans and a little strappy top, with optional sparkly bits (then again, it was the 1990s). It was easy, versatile and, looking back on it, really quite dull: we all stuck to that same theme. A combination of *Sex and the City*, the enormous variation and often frivolous party clothes that suddenly were on offer, and having more spare cash and confidence changed all that. Dresses and skirts are now what the girl about town are seen in. Nina, a former colleague at Thomas Pink, thinks nothing of wearing sequins to work. As the only woman working in the IT department, she was always a breath of fresh air, glamour being in fairly short supply in that particular room. I love that attitude: life is too short not to sparkle at your desk.

As the saying goes, you never get a second chance to make a first impression. However, I was lucky, I did get a second chance to make a good impression. I first met Rupert at the age of seventeen on a cricket pitch. He was in cricket whites, which was entirely appropriate given he was one of the players, while I was in cut-off Levi 501s and a blue floral blouse. He looked like he had come off the set of *Brideshead Revisited* and was extremely handsome. He didn't give me a second glance – he was more interested in the cricket. As for me, well I was more interested in his best friend.

Fast-forward twenty-three years and here we were, going on a date. I was beside myself with nerves in case he did ultimately decide I was every bit as daft, annoying and immature as he'd found me all those years ago. I wanted to look grown up, stylish and, above all, as if I hadn't put too much thought into getting ready. Phew! In the end the weather swayed it for me, at least I would be appropriately dressed for the cold January air. I went with my smartest Seven jeans: expensive, flattering and free, courtesy of a mystery-shopping assignment, thank you very much. Besides, a little black dress might have seemed a tad over the top for the local bar we were meeting in. High-heeled boots on a winter's night are a confidence-boosting, leg-lengthening no-brainer, as long as you can still walk in them after a bottle of Pinot Grigio. I arrived first which was unusual in itself, and looked impatiently at my watch until Rupert strolled in, wrapped up in a navy duffel coat which made him look even younger than he already did. I was nervous and I suspected he might be too but after a couple of drinks he asked if I'd eaten (of course I hadn't) and from then on it was as if we'd known each other forever.

Rupert texted to suggest dinner, a third date in fact, should anyone be counting . . .

2013 was revving up; it was time for a shift of gear.

CHAPTER ELEVEN

A Pair of Vegetarian Sandals

R upert and I were in the unusual position of being able to spend time together every other weekend when our two small children were with their other parents. It was an odd thing, to be parents and yet doing things that single people do, without the time constraint or cost of babysitters. We were lucky in that respect. All those things that get pushed out because they never even make it to the middle of the list of priorities when you have a child in tow – the trips to the cinema, the lazy Sunday brunches, the impromptu shopping excursions – we were able to do, and because we had both missed doing those things we did them all. It was a slow and cautious start, which I sometimes found frustrating (I'm an 'all or nothing' kinda girl, while even that expression irritates Rupert), but as we already knew each other's history and had a good few friends in common, that was a couple of conversations ticked off the list. It was almost like a relationship you might have in your twenties, only with two children already in existence and fewer fashion mistakes.

He hasn't changed much in twenty-six years, at least not when it comes to clothes. Rupert, I discovered, still had a thing for expensive coats, although he did occasionally take them off now – and I even persuaded him to venture back to the house in Kingston.

We are excellent shopping companions. Rupert comes in, picks things out, gives an opinion at the fitting room and is tireless on a quest to locate exactly the right piece. Both single parents with budgets, we are competitive about our bargain hunting. He is perhaps even better at finding gems on the clearance rail at TK Maxx than I am, such is his knowledge of niche brands.

Not too many bargains to be had in Northcote Road in Battersea, where I live. It's commonly known as 'Nappy Valley'. To walk down Northcote Road without a pram, a visible pregnancy, or both, is to look like you have accidentally taken a wrong turn on your way to Battersea Rise or St John's Hill nearby, both haunts of the young, free and single. If you do happen to see a group of teenagers or an old person, you have to assume they are part of some kind of babysitting consortium.

I have lived in the area since moving to St John's Hill in 1997, when the proximity of a Cafe Rouge and a late-night newsagent was essential. On the birth of my son in 2010 I moved to Northcote Road, where the two 'Outstanding' schools, the plethora of cafes and the wealth of outdoor space with playgrounds makes family life there somewhat idyllic. Naturally all this comes with a price: it is no coincidence that independent designer boutiques, cocktail bars and specialist childrenswear shops thrive here.

Despite the appearance of many of the shops, the countless estate agents and the over-enthusiastic parking wardens, Northcote Road has a villagey atmosphere where people are friendly. Due to what seems like a permanent baby boom – indeed this area reportedly has the highest number of babies and toddlers in Europe – children are usually tolerated, if not always appreciated. There are many areas like this in London. The child-centric shopping experience is becoming more mainstream and the hole in the retail market once pasted over by Mothercare and Boots is now being properly filled by the likes of Trotters, JoJo Maman and pregnancy-wear specialist Seraphina – all three are permanent fixtures of Northcote Road alongside Whistles, Space NK, Jack Wills and LK Bennett.

Specialist shops focusing on a very particular part of the market aren't exactly new: in Battersea we have had a honey shop, a cheese shop, a door shop and a sewing machine shop for years. However, those springing up now take it to a different level – in Northcote Road the meringue shop and the decorate-your-own biscuit shop make honey and doors suddenly seem very last century.

*

Many of the parents who live in and shop on Northcote Road are conscious of shopping ethically and choosing products made from sustainable materials. But Jodi Zervos of Merino Kids feels that the UK has been slow to catch on to the idea of sustainable fashion compared to somewhere like New Zealand, where it has been a way of life for many years. Even now, the benefits of natural fabrics such as merino and cashmere versus the man-made fabrics more commonly used in so-called 'fast fashion' are not generally high on consumers' lists of priorities. But surely things are changing?

After many years at Office London, Sean Farrell worked as a consultant for the Natural Shoe Store, an offshoot of Birkenstock and one of the few retailers who have made a business out of vegetarian, organic footwear.

'There is a market for it,' says Sean, 'but it's very niche [still]. The Natural Shoe Store have built up a customer base over the years. It's a nice sideline, but unlike the shoes, it's not really sustainable as the focal point of a business.'

How does such a brand exist then in this day and age, especially with austerity measures and poverty affecting more people than ever before? It's not as if being green and socially responsible isn't a costly business in itself. The cost of sustainable fibres is substantially higher and in the end who should pay for that extra cost, the retailer or the consumer?

'The Natural Shoe Store survives because its parent company is Birkenstock UK,' states Sean, before adding with more than a measure of irony, 'and Birkenstocks were huge last year . . .' I feel guilty laughing about it but Sean is not someone I can imagine running around in vegetarian shoes. Sean wears Hudson and Superga, we're not talking about your run-of-the-mill Crocs and Superdry-wearing dad here.

However, many of the high-street chains have started to look at a garment's life cycle. H&M is just one example (but probably the most high-profile one) of a high-street name producing sustainable collections every season. These garments made out of hemp, organic linen and organic leather have more of a limited-edition vibe. H&M have marketed their 'Conscious' collection through high-profile ad campaigns featuring well-known faces – including actress Olivia Wilde and most recently Julia Restoin Roitfeld – which helps to shift the emphasis from worthy to desirable: it's all very well producing an eco-friendly collection but it's pointless if nobody wants to buy it. Unfortunately the words 'vegan', 'non-toxic', 'organic' and 'fairtrade' conjure up a non-glamorous image of the early dull, scratchy, unfashionable clothes in muted colours, whereas the reality is now very different.

Since 2013, H&M is also the place to go with all your unwanted clothes and textiles, which you can swap for a five-pound-off voucher for use in their stores; their sister store & Other Stories offers a 10 per cent discount on the return of their cosmetics containers. H&M's policy is 'Rewear, Reuse, Recycle', meaning if the clothes handed in can't be marketed as second-hand goods then they will be converted into other products, such as cleaning cloths, and if even that can't be done then the textiles will be turned into raw materials and used to produce energy. The goal at H&M is zero waste, and in addition to the customer incentive they promise that for each kilo of textiles they collect, 0.02 euros will be donated to a local charitable organisation chosen by H&M: the British Red Cross in the UK; UNICEF in their homeland of Sweden. At H&M their aim is to be using only sustainable cotton by 2020. The Swedish brand, however, is streets ahead of others in this respect. Indeed it was the first to sign the legally binding Bangladesh Safety Accord following the tragic events in Dhaka in 2013 – the collapse of the unregulated Rana Plaza factory building, which killed over a thousand garment workers, brought a previously, and perhaps conveniently, ignored issue to the forefront for many retailers.

Meanwhile, ASOS Africa, which promotes growth and empowerment and encourages artisan producers all across Africa, has quietly produced their eleventh collection. Marks and Spencer has joined forces with Colin Firth's wife Livia, an eco-fashion activist who founded the Green Carpet Challenge, a mission to bring vintage, Fairtrade and ethically sourced fashion to red-carpet events. In putting together her collection for M&S, she spent time at ranches in Brazil where they address deforestation and sustainability through a ground-breaking programme that teaches ranchers to be green. As a result of Livia's campaign, Meryl Streep picked up her 2012 Oscar for *The Iron Lady* in a gold Lanvin dress made from recycled plastic bottles.

Thomas Pink's Holly Browne started her career working for the production department at Ted Baker. Part of her job was liaising with and then making regular visits to the factories based in Turkey and Portugal. When a Ted Baker colleague commented that Holly was lucky as she was getting to travel to 'the nice factories', she started to ask questions, what was meant by 'nice' factories and what was wrong with the other factories that were allegedly not so nice? By 2010 she had created a new role for herself as Ted Baker's 'Green Guardian', looking at sustainability the whole way through the supply chain.

Monsoon, which started life in 1973 from a stall in London's Portobello Road, is a brand known for its products sourced from the Far East, India and Afghanistan. Monsoon's design team continues to find inspiration from all around the world and is committed to ethical trading. The company's compliance team regularly checks their factories are abiding by its code of conduct, which sets out minimum requirements on working conditions, pay and employment rights.

Boden CEO Johnnie Boden travels regularly with his design team to the factories in India where much of their product is manufactured, as does Fred Willems, head of design at Thomas Pink working alongside Holly Browne, whose job title is the utterly ambiguous-sounding 'supplier compliance co-ordinator'. Thomas Pink still have some small factories in the UK and, says Holly, on the occasions where they have visited the factories to carry out audits, the factory management are bewildered by their questions because they've never been audited in this way before.

'There's always something new to think of,' Holly says, 'from the amount of energy we use at head office to what we do with shirts at the end of their life.' In addition to the 2012 Energy Efficiency Directive (a set of binding measures to help the EU reach its 20 per cent energy efficiency target by 2020), since 2015 businesses have had to make public their efforts to stop the use of slave labour by its suppliers.

It would be wrong to assume that factory conditions are purely a problem for the more affordable end of the high street. CEO of H&M Karl-Johan Persson, who took over the role from his father Stefan in 2009, argues that high-cost brands were as much a part of the problem as so-called fast-fashion stores. In an interview in the *Financial Times* in May 2013 he stated, 'The salaries for the workers are the same, regardless of the price the customer gets. The margins are different. We see medium to luxury brands in the same factory but they charge 10, 20, 100 times more. So you shouldn't only look at the final price.'

Stella McCartney, a lifelong vegetarian who never uses leather or fur in her collections, has been the most vocal and actively progressive on this subject, but otherwise the world of high fashion has been dragging its feet. A cynical soul might suggest that where once the subject of sustainable and ethical style was unsexy, now it is an opportunity and one that ultimately no fashion house can afford to waste.

The biggest issue of all is the pace of Planet Fashion itself. By its very nature, high fashion lasts a season at most and then we are encouraged, if not coerced, to move on to the next collection less than six months later. The life cycle of most fashion is short-lived. It remains to be seen if the current appetite for sustainability is, ultimately, sustainable.

It's no coincidence that 'vintage' pieces have grown in popularity from the days when sourcing your clothes from charity shops was the domain of the frugal student. Now everyone from award-nominated film stars to burlesque performers are known for their vintage style. When I was interviewing the guests as they walked up the red carpet at the BAFTAs in 2007, none was more eye-catching in blood red Dior than French actress and Bond Girl Eva Green. As I chatted to her about how she chose her gown for the event, I could see that it was so old the fabric was covered in tiny pulls. Eva, who won the rising star award that night, had crazy backcombed hair and a laid-back confidence and she utterly pulled off the look.

There are many different reasons to bring environmentalism and social responsibility to the manufacturing of the clothes that we buy – kindness to animals is one issue, while the tightening of labour laws overseas is quite another. The answer is educating people but there is still a long way to go. For example, I had no idea that the farming of organic cotton uses less water, no pesticides and has lower carbon emissions, which goes towards reducing the carbon footprint. According to Levi's, over 3,000 litres of water will be used during the full product lifecycle of a single pair of 501 jeans, from the cotton production and manufacturing process to their regular washing at home. Reducing this water consumption through the use of organic cotton is costly, though, because the cotton has to be segregated and that means different transport costs and extra manpower.

In her book *Why Fashion Matters*, author and head of the London College of Fashion Frances Corner suggests, 'If we all extended the use of a garment by nine months – which according to studies would mean making it last three years – we would save $8 billion a year on the cost of resources used to manufacture, launder and dispose of clothing. The carbon, water and waste footprints of our clothes would be reduced by 20 to 30 per cent. Surely nine months isn't too much to ask?'

Well no, it isn't, especially when you consider that jeans were first produced as hardwearing workwear, built to withstand far more than the average molly-coddled pair of jeans these days.

However, my sister-in-law Lucy, who has worked in the fashion industry for over twelve years, and now runs her own company Brand Ambassadors, which supplies clothing brands to independent boutiques, isn't convinced the public will pay more for socially responsible products: 'Consumers just don't care enough about sustainability and the desire for cheap clothing is too strong.' She feels that while a small number of consumers may boycott a given shop or brand if they are reported to have unethical working conditions, most don't know or care what the difference is between say, organic cotton and regular non-organic cotton.

Melanie Traub of Secret Sales is equally emphatic on the subject. 'The consumer is still more interested in newness and price than sustainability and there is no sign of this changing.'

Maybe we simply don't care enough in this country. As Merino Kids' Jodi sums up, 'In New Zealand we have this beautiful landscape that we love and want to protect so sustainability is part of our way of life.' Jodi is characteristically diplomatic in concluding, 'It's just different in the UK.'

The charge of 5p for plastic bags is a mere drop in the ocean. I have a cotton bag in my car alongside my umbrella, but do I ever remember to take either one with me when there is a potential need? To date, no. I haven't. I live in hope. After all, I didn't used to remember my small child and mobile phone when I left the house each day, but I do now, almost always.

Away from the 'local' shopping streets, the British high street is the place to go for those established stalwarts whose appeal is across the board, incorporating everyone from babies to grandparents. The lines separating childhood, teenage and young adult blur further and further and the benchmark for what is 'middle age' and 'old age' is no longer relevant. H&M, Zara, Monsoon, Office, Benetton and Uniqlo offer products for the whole family, with little or no distinction between which collection is intended for which adult age group. I have shopped in H&M with my grandmother, my mum, my boyfriend, my best friends and our various children, sometimes all at the same time, it really can be a one-stop shopping destination and there's nothing more handy than that. Richard Cristofoli has been in retail for over twenty years. He says the Debenhams customer is between thirty-five and fifty-four with an average age of forty-six. 'However,' Richard clarifies, 'we prefer to think of our customers in terms of attitude and mindset rather than age because forty-six is just not the same as it was in previous generations. The Debenhams shopper is more fashion-oriented, we say they refuse to give up on fashion.'

H&M goes from strength to strength. I don't think there's another brand like it. I have visited H&M branches all over the world, I can't help myself, but nowhere was more exciting than Stockholm, the home of Hennes & Mauritz. When I visited with Rupert, our first trip there, I imagined there would be an H&M on every street corner much like the Benettons in Italy and the Gaps in America in the 1990s.

We flew to Stockholm from Heathrow and while Rupert went off to buy himself a newspaper, I told him I was going for a look around duty free and would meet him at the checkout.

Rupert was always, like many, bewildered by my ambition to be an actress, as he finds the idea of getting up on stage absolutely horrendous. Which is why I didn't tell him I would be earning a quick buck in duty free. Well, why not? I was passing through anyway, and what was a couple of questions about body lotion going to hurt? I would engage the assistant and be done and paying for the YSL Touche Eclat I genuinely needed before he knew what was going on.

To be fair, Rupert has never complained about such things, but he does like to be on time. On the other hand, I have always left everything to the last minute and have been known to run the entire distance from departure lounge to gate, hurling myself through the aircraft doors just as they are closing.

I raced to the designer beauty area. Rupert, who had re-joined me far quicker than I had allowed for, immediately started to chivvy me along. Initially I ignored him, hoping he wouldn't overhear the nonsense I was coming out with about my mum's birthday (still five months away) and all manner of imagined skin conditions. But of course he did and started to look at his watch.

'Come on, can't you do this another time? How much longer are you going to be? Have you got what you needed?'

I knew the game was up so I brought the transaction to a close as quickly as possible. An airport branch is the one place where the closing statement, 'Thanks so much for your help, I'm going to think about it and then come back,' is probably its least convincing.

Stockholm was just as I'd hoped, at least five branches of H&M within walking distance from our hotel and we went in every single one of them. Bliss.

H&M isn't the only Swedish brand to create ripples here in the UK. Cos (short for Collection Of Style), which launched in 2007 overseen by Karl-Johan Persson, now CEO of H&M, and & Other Stories joining it on Regent Street in 2013, both hail from the same stable as H&M, and they have made their mark with their visually stimulating stores offering not just clothes but a whole lifestyle. Cos has a minimal approach to their designs with an emphasis on the angular, a kind of sartorial version of IKEA while the & Other Stories branches are a glorious mixture of a girly boudoir full of delicious-smelling lotions and a fashion shoot. They are targeting slightly different markets but rarely do any of the three charge more than £100 for anything, even a cashmere sweater.

There is something about these Scandinavian brands that leave you wanting more. Is it the incredible attention to detail? Or is it the mixture of basics, designer copies and stylish classic pieces, and the sheer choice of it, that means there is something for everyone, regardless of age or style?

Persson says that he tries to stay true to the mindset of his grandfather, founder of H&M, Erling Persson, who had an informal management style that focused on long-term results. It is safe to say, the strategy is working, in 2013 H&M listed its annual revenue as over $150 billion.

For every H&M, Sports Direct, Kurt Geiger, Reiss and TK Maxx, which continue to open new branches each year, there is a Knickerbox, Ravel, Barratt's, Woolworth's and Comet, all of which have disappeared from our high streets. But despite the closure of many of Britain's stores in recent years, the quality and quantity of goods turned over in our town centres is high. UK fashion is the best in the world with cutting-edge trends making the transition from catwalk to sidewalk faster than ever before and, what's more, at affordable prices. The imports that once were unique to London's West End shopping meccas are now a familiar sight out of town too.

The competition has never been more fierce and with that comes the mystery shopper, who not only keeps staff on their toes but can also be used to find out just what it is exactly that the competition are offering down the road. Fashion chains are having to look beyond what has previously been expected of the in-store experience and in doing so have followed the example of the more high-end brands for whom service has always been a priority. No longer are the staff on the shop floor referred to as shop assistants or sales associates, now they are personal shoppers or stylists who are as likely to offer you refreshments as they are to take a measurement.

The preppy American brands, Abercrombie & Fitch, which first came to London in 2007, along with Hollister and Gilly Hicks (the latter closing in 2014), made their name hiring so-called 'models' (the shop-floor staff) to work in their branches with shirtless males often seen posing in the entrance. The A&F brief was for staff to exude 'aloofness' to the largely teenage customers. The stores themselves were dark and loud, the clothes pricey and heavily branded. Since 2015 Abercrombie & Fitch have adjusted their policy to focus less on the sexy staff, now called 'Brand Representatives', and various legal conflicts over their employment practices have prompted an about-turn in their customer-service ethic. Still, it's interesting that this brand, like the British equivalent Jack Wills, aimed at school children and young adults, sells college-style clothes with very adult price tags, the kind of thing that didn't exist when I was in sixth form. We shopped at Miss Selfridge and Chelsea Girl and there really wasn't an alternative, not on the high street anyway. Perhaps the point is more that the emphasis with these brands is on quality and investment, with the well-sourced fabrics more likely to last the whole three years of an average university course, the antithesis of the Primark style of disposable fast fashion.

It doesn't pay to be aloof or stand-offish towards consumers in this day and age, not when there are so many thousands of mystery shoppers lurking on every shop floor. The customer has to feel welcomed, valued and should be invited back at the very least, and that means making small talk, asking questions, offering suggestions and additional items: in a nutshell, Going The Extra Mile. Really, the only way to be absolutely sure of scoring highly with the undercover shopper is by endeavouring to score highly with every customer every day – just in case, because you may think you've spotted the suspicious-looking character who appears to be paying a lot of attention to detail, but can you be totally sure?

Jessica Burnham worked for Marks and Spencer for nine years and during that time mystery shopping was carried out on a monthly basis. She describes it as 'a big deal at M&S' with rewards coming in the form of £50 vouchers for staff who performed well. Jessica says it wasn't obvious to staff who the mystery shoppers were so sales assistants tended to treat everyone as if they were a mystery shopper. This practice alone is an effective way to raise the customer service to a new level.

'They didn't name and shame the customer assistance that scored badly,' she says, 'instead they were taken aside and micro-managed with targets. They were then revisited weeks later with the hope that their attention to detail with every customer improved!'

Was the service today beyond your expectations? Now there's the million-dollar question because what do we expect from service in this day and age? Even now I don't expect much from a high-street store: politeness, a smile, an extra till to be opened up if the queue is starting to stretch. But then I'm a confident shopper, I don't need to be approached or hassled with offers of help because I am more than happy to wander and browse for hours. I like to think I know what looks good on me and what doesn't, but I also have a good idea of what will and won't work on most people. I'm the sort of person who accompanies a friend on a shopping trip and then treads on the toes of all the shop assistants with my suggestions.

When the penny finally dropped that perhaps I could make this advice official, turn what I happily spent hours doing for fun and relaxation into an actual career, it was as if a light had been switched on.

There is a massive choice on the British high street, too much choice, in the opinion of fashion commentator Eric Musgrave. Choice can be overwhelming, I get that: I fly into a panic when faced with choosing a pizza topping. The answer is to narrow down the choice and you do that by asking yourself three questions:

What is your colour palette?

What is your body shape?

What is your lifestyle?

When you have the answers to these questions, you may still not know how or where to shop but you will automatically cut out a lot of unsuitable items you may previously have wasted time considering in the past.

*

In the same way you might say a rude word quietly if a small child is in ear shot, so I was careful not to say the words 'mystery shopping' in front of my increasingly articulate son Jake, knowing he would be bound to ask what it meant.

But it was only a matter of time. One day you go on a quite innocent post-Christmas look at the sales with aforementioned child in tow, you both enter Monsoon in Kingston-upon-Thames and he looks around and asks at the top of his voice, 'Mummy, are we mystery shopping now?' It's then that you know your days as a mystery shopper are numbered.

With Jake almost at the age for full-time education, I had started to slightly freak out about how fast time was flying. Motherhood was more rewarding than I could have imagined, but once Jake started at school I would be restricted in what I could do workwise. When an advert for a colour analysis course caught my eye on Groupon one day, I decided to give it a go. If I didn't like it, at least I would have had my colours done and would know which worked best on me. If it turned out to be a good fit, then I could look into doing further courses. I was genuinely excited: I'd booked my course, spoken to Nisha Hunjan, the founder of Style ME who was running the course, and she was enthusiastic about the various ways I was already involved in fashion. As I entered my forties, after a decade of such enormous highs and lows, I felt quietly confident, wondering what this next chapter – the one when life reportedly begins – might bring.

Nisha showed me how pale pink and baby blue would play down the shadows on my face while navy and dark brown were far less ageing than black. To be honest, I wasn't thrilled to hear that baby colours, and the green *ER* doctors' scrubs, were ideal for me. But since then I've found they are the fastest way to have people commenting on how well I look. So, I've wiped away the tears and mentally put all the black away for good.

Once back home, I went through my many clothes asking myself questions about why I was holding on to some pieces, why others were well-worn favourites and why some hadn't even had the labels removed. There was a range of answers from loving the style of something to being attached to an item of clothing because my dad had once said he liked the colour. I had so many clothes and yet more often than not I would stand in front of them overwhelmed at the choice and at a loss for something to wear. The idea of clearing out, making space, assessing what was good and what wasn't and then starting over with some rules in place, was hugely exciting and I couldn't wait to get started with my own heaving wardrobes.

In mystery-shopping guise, I had to be the shopper that wants and needs assistance. It was a funny thing to be doing and sometimes I wondered how on earth it came to pass that I almost spent more time shopping incognito than I did as myself. Now the shoe was on the other foot. I would be the one offering the help and maybe, if I really put my mind to it, I could get paid for it too.

∽

HOW TO DETOX YOUR WARDROBE

Do you dream of a streamlined closet with colour coordinated pieces that complement each other, hanging elegantly with space in between each hanger? I know I do. Imagine being safe in the knowledge that every item in that wardrobe looks good, fits well and feels comfortable. Wouldn't it be amazing to have a walk-in wardrobe where you can instantly observe all your shoes, belts and bags? Just think how much time you'd save in the morning. Does such a thing even exist beyond the confines of Pinterest, Instagram and the Kardashian household?

Most of us have too much stuff and not enough space to store it. It's why storage facilities have sprung up all over the place, unit upon unit filled with the belongings we have no room for in our day-to-day lives, can clearly live without but just can't face parting with once and for all.

Many of us, to some degree, use our clothes as a security blanket. We hold on to garments and shoes long past their sell-by date for when we're thinner, or bigger, or pregnant again, or (and this is my favourite, cited mostly by men) 'for doing the decorating in'. It's an emotional thing, we attach a great deal to what's in our wardrobe and there are many people I've spoken to, both men and women, who are reluctant to get rid of things simply because it feels too painful to do so. This is completely normal. But then I would say that, I'm a repeat offender. I have a long black coat I haven't worn for years but can't bear to part with it because my dad bought it for me – he didn't actually choose it, you understand, he simply gave me the money, but still. I've never liked goodbyes.

Clinical hoarding – where sufferers store up stuff to the detriment of their health and safety – is more serious. 'Pathological collecting' to give it the correct medical label, is a serious medical condition. So if you are reading this book by candlelight in a small space you have carved out of floor-to-ceiling shoe boxes, newspapers dating back to the last century and mountains of stuffed-full carrier bags, you are someone for whom the ability to discard is completely absent. I'm afraid I'm not qualified to help with that.

I do love a good wardrobe detox though, and never more so than when it's someone else's stuff. It's so much simpler without the emotional attachment and, after all, who doesn't love a nose through someone else's cupboards? I know it's hard, I really do, change can be horrible, but it can also be very liberating. Aside from which, if you clear space, there will be room for new things!

Here are my tips for a successful declutter:

1. Aim to declutter your wardrobe twice a year. It may be stating the obvious but the start of a new season is the best time to get into the frame of mind of: out with the old and in with the new. The new collections are in the shops and you can promise yourself a shopping trip if you have a good clear out.

2. Be honest with yourself. You've heard the theory about 20 per cent of your wardrobe being worn 80 per cent of the time, right? This is because we buy or hold on to things which are no longer relevant to our lives – clothes which no longer fit or are unsuitable for our current lifestyle. I found myself on maternity leave with a rail full of cocktail dresses and at least fifty pairs of stilettos. I had nothing suitable for sitting around breastfeeding, or bouncing Jake in his chair with my foot while eating cake, which seemed to be all I did for the first month. Things change, bodies change, it's all an excuse to go shopping as far as I'm concerned. With several shops offering incentives for bagfuls of unwanted garments for recycling and eBay at your fingertips, you could even be quids in.

3. Only keep what you absolutely love. Make three piles; one for things to definitely keep, one for items to be recycled or taken to the charity shop and one for those you're not sure about. It's the 'undecided' pile which is the dangerous one, so this is where being ruthless kicks in. Anything which doesn't fit perfectly or isn't absolutely flattering has to go – don't ever keep anything

because you think you'll slim into it. If you do dras-
tically lose weight you should reward yourself with
something new at the very least! Equally, any pieces
which are stained, ripped, holey or frayed should be
transferred to the 'bin it' pile. Those pieces which have
nostalgic value are the hardest to part with I know. I
still have a smiley face T-shirt with '1989' printed across
the chest simply because that was the really hot summer
the year before A levels when I met my dearest friends.
I'll probably still have that top when I die.

4. Throw away all wire hangers. I hate those things – even
    if they do come free with your drycleaning. Nothing
    thrives on a wire hanger. Jackets will keep their shape
    far better on a thick wooden hanger and smart skirts
    and trousers are best on hangers too. Knitwear should
    always be folded. If it is being packed away for the
    summer it should be stored in air-tight bags that provide
    a defence against the evil moths. Although on that note,
    moths today don't seem to have the high standards of
    their forefathers and will eat through any old fabric, not
    just the cashmere and merino.

5. Take a hard line on underwear. Think with the mindset
    of someone in the first throes of a new romance. Would
    I want to pose in the bedroom doorway in this slightly
    bagging pair of nylon briefs with not quite matching
    flesh-coloured bra? If the answer is no then bung it.
    Greying knickers with dubious elasticity are not 'period
    pants', they will make you feel worse, if anything, and

deserve to be retired. Ditto uncomfortable or unflattering bras. Tights which are not completely intact are an accident waiting to happen, you'll curse yourself when some nice young man points out you have a ladder, so bin those too.

6. Get your colours done. Knowing which shades are best for you will cut out those that aren't, which will save you time, money and space in the long run. Wearing the right colours will make you look more fabulous and that will put a spring in your step. It's also cheaper than Botox and doesn't need doing more than once in your life – how's that for an investment?

7. Feet change size too, and scruffy old shoes and boots look rubbish. Don't keep footwear because they used to be something great and they may come back into fashion one day. They probably will, but everything comes back with a twist. Trust me, next time round they won't work.

8. Maintain good habits. For every new thing you buy discard at least one, if not two, old pieces, so you don't slip back into your old ways. You could try that trick of turning around your hanger each time you wear the item on it, so you can see which things haven't been worn for six months – but do you really have the time for that? It is perfectly acceptable to wear something to death for one season and then be sick of the sight of it the next. Clothes should make you happy: if you don't love it, leave it.

.

CHAPTER TWELVE

The Off-the-Shoulder Dress from Paris

I n 2015, the mystery shopping industry was estimated to be worth $1.5 billion with an estimated 1.5 million people employed by it worldwide. Mystery Shoppers, a market research company founded in 1991, reports having a database of over 200,000 shoppers on its books. The thousands of mystery shoppers are keeping watch, listening intently and taking it all in. The woman standing next to you may look like a normal customer but that's not a shopping list she's checking, it's a set of instructions, and she isn't texting her mum, she's making a note of the name of the staff member who has forgotten to ask if there is anything else she needs.

When I was first asked to record a mystery-shopping visit to a high-street building society, I was taken aback. I was sent a package containing a small recording device the like of which my dad used when he was a reporter on the *Daily Mirror*. It all felt very furtive. Now there is an increasing demand for mystery shoppers who own their own video recording equipment, which has to be covert – videoing the transaction on a mobile phone just won't do, and the equipment available now to the average consumer is worthy of James Bond. Most companies are keen to implement this growing area of the industry and shoppers with their own equipment, which can often be purchased through the research company's own website, earn a bigger fee.

But this is where I draw the line. The member of staff is paid to do a job to the best of their ability, and so are mystery shoppers: recording the event puts the mystery shopper under scrutiny almost as much as the staff member. I have made mistakes or forgotten to ask pertinent questions now and again. When you have to remember names, descriptions, what was said, how it was said, the number of light bulbs that may or may not have been out, whether promotional material was displayed properly, if the door was open or shut, if the opening hours were displayed and how many minutes you waited to be served, well, it's a big ask to get it all perfect every time.

Ed Hoskins has been a pub landlord for eight years and is used to 'mystery diners', as they are labelled in the hospitality sector. Usually sent by the brewery to which the pub is attached, the outcome of the reports, which has to be an astonishing 97 per cent or above throughout the year, affects bonuses. Ed's pubs (there have been five over the years) are popular eateries in affluent areas of London. He explains that it's not always the company head office employing the mystery diners. Sometimes the reports might be sponsored by a brand with an interest, for example a lager company wanting to check their lager is being served in the correct branded glass and at the right temperature.

'We have mystery diners once a quarter,' says Ed. 'Sometimes you can spot the them, it all depends on the type of pub. If it's not the kind of pub where customers book a table for two midweek and then spend sixty pounds on a slap-up lunch with wine then you have a fairly good idea they might be that month's mystery diner. In a pub which is a popular lunch destination for local businesses then it's not so obvious.'

It has to be said that a £60 budget is extremely generous for a pub-lunch assignment and it's far more usual to have £15 that 'goes towards' your bill. Rupert and I once reported on a hotel restaurant, one with a famous chef attached, and were reimbursed £120 for the pleasure, but this was highly unusual, as was the experience itself, it has to be said.

It took me a year to tell Rupert I was a mystery shopper. In the end, I divulged my secret as I needed someone to accompany me on a lunchtime assignment near to where he lives. He was more than happy to share a free lunch, but the whole concept made him feel very uncomfortable. He simply didn't feel good about scoring hard-working, low-paid people. He encouraged me to score highly even if I wasn't convinced. It is an interesting stance, given that in a genuine dining out situation he has very high standards. He would have no qualms avoiding somewhere he felt had under-performed. Not offered a drink within five minutes of being seated? Rupert won't stand for that and, generally speaking, neither will the restaurant business.

Timings are another essential detail that the management of the food and drink industry are keen to test. Thank god for mobile phones! When I started in this business, mobile phones were far more basic than those we use now. Having a stopwatch with a lap function on the same gadget that you could use to log all the information in note form, take photographs with and then enter all the results on to was a game-changer.

It may be a good incentive to have staff you trust to do a decent job most of the time, but frustrating if as a manager you feel the report unfairly represents a staff member, and here a video recording of the whole experience could be beneficial.

'It has happened that reports are blatantly made up and in that case we contest it,' says Ed. 'It's immediately obvious when the mystery diner is just in it for a free meal because the report is so inaccurate.'

Ed is a laid-back husband and father with a good sense of humour, but it's not hard to imagine that for some without his confidence or paycheque, difficult feedback could be hard to take.

What does and doesn't constitute good customer service varies enormously on who you ask. I cringed inwardly when I was asked for my first name in a sportswear retailer so the assistant could then use it repeatedly as if we were close pals, before closing the interaction by asking how I felt the service had been today. The honest answer would be that I felt embarrassed by the staff member asking for my personal details, and desperately sorry for her having to request feedback on the service. For me, this constant probing is a sure-fire way to ensure I don't return to the shop. I know I'm not alone in preferring to be left to my own devices until I am ready to ask for help.

If the mystery-shopping companies are upping their game and asking more and more of their agents, then it is only in response to the ever-more-attentive customer service. Champagne in Jimmy Choo, chocolates in Oliver Bonas, samples in L'Occitane, it's all par for the course nowadays.

Over a decade of mystery-shopping experience came to a head when last year I went on my most illustrious assignment yet: an extremely high-end independent watchmaker was rolling out a programme to test the service at their Sloane Street boutique. But this was no ordinary visit because I was to make a purchase at the end of it. In order to facilitate this spend, a credit card was issued in my name with a £30,000 spend limit. Oh, the things that went through my mind when that arrived in the post! A fortnight in the Caribbean? A new car? I could actually purchase some of those incredible clothes and shoes I'd tried on at so many exclusive outlets. After hundreds of mystery-shopping reports had left me feeling slightly jaded about the whole business, suddenly the adrenalin kicked back in.

What on earth was I going to wear? It took me an hour to find the right combination for a shopping trip for a luxury watch. I picked out my camel coat from Zara (initially bought to accommodate huge breastfeeding boobs but surprisingly versatile after the event too, as it turned out) and accessorised with a leopard-print scarf, which could have been an expensive designer silk scarf but definitely wasn't. The *pièce de résistance* was a pair of stiletto-heeled suede shoes, the D&G ones that always make me smile because they came into my life just before Jake. Despite a long debate with myself over which shoes were the most appropriate for the task at hand, I regretted those shoes after the sprint to the station resulted in painful feet before the day had hardly even begun. As I hobbled down Sloane Street a window display caught my eye. Staring longingly at the beautiful sequin gown in the window of Escada, I checked my teeth and smoothed down my hair for the umpteenth time and told myself

I looked fine and that with the right attitude any outfit could be passed off as expensive.

Once I'd been let through the security doors onto the shop floor, holding my head high as if this was second nature, I felt the nerves slip away. It helped that half an hour before I had been a few doors down trying on Italian designer coats costing over £1,000. I'd warmed into the role and now felt I could afford to buy my husband a watch worth more than I earn in a year. Really good staff are polite and friendly to every single person who walks through the door, no matter what their appearance and intention and this occasion was no different. I was quickly scooped up, offered a beverage (tea, coffee or mineral water – no champagne here interestingly, disappointingly) and showed to a seat at a desk in the corner.

Now this was a worrying development. Had I blown my cover? Was I being hidden away out of sight because of my Zara coat or was it the annoying kink in my long hair that had appeared the minute it started to drizzle? The hushed tones of the staff and their terribly solemn customers raised the tension. I am a person who is inclined to make jokes and laugh a little too loudly, so this kind of environment can put me on edge. Luckily I also have enough acting experience to know that if you pretend to be something quite different, you will usually get away with it. Even so, I really should have rehearsed what to say when asked what watch my husband currently wears.

'Has your husband bought one of our watches before, Mrs Stott?' enquired the charming salesperson.

'No, but he has often mentioned wanting one, which was why I knew this would be a lovely surprise for his fortieth birthday,' I said, picturing my perfect thirty-nine-year-old imaginary husband.

'Absolutely, and this particular model is the perfect watch to start with. What watch does he wear currently, if you don't mind me asking?'

(Shit. What watch does Rupert wear? He was going on about it just yesterday and I haven't a clue. Oh god, how could I be so stupid? SAY SOMETHING QUICKLY!)

'He has a Tag Heuer he's had for many years. He's very sentimental about it.'

(Totally made that up.)

'Yes, of course. So your husband prefers a sporty-style watch then?'

(And suddenly I'm into the swing of it.)

'Actually he's quite classic in his style, he appreciates beautiful things, but he isn't into fussy details or anything too elaborate . . .'

And so it went on. As mystery-shopping visits go, this one was quite exhausting; I earned my money, that's for sure. Not knowing very much about watches was almost less of a problem than imagining myself as someone with a husband on whom I wished to spend £28,000.

When the moment came and this wealthy housewife decided to take the plunge and buy the watch, the process of payment began. Still no champagne offered, I noted. Clearly, spending several thousand pounds on one item is simply what you do in this establishment, it's not cause for celebration.

The rather attractive and impeccably coiffured female assistant remained charming and patient throughout the transaction with no suggestion she was not convinced by my story. Somebody had to sit in the corner and it just so happened that, because the other desks were occupied, that person was me. After an hour and a half of scrutiny and keeping my language and mannerisms in check, I was not only knackered but also famished and in grave need of a coffee. I was escorted to the security doors, asked if I would like a cab (I decline, after all I'm hot-footing it to Costa for a cappuccino and ham-and-cheese toastie, not lunching at Scott's) and then she hands me the loot.

'Thank you, Mrs Stott. Enjoy the rest of your day. We will put the certificate of ownership in the post to your husband today,' said the assistant with a warm smile. 'I'm sure your husband will be thrilled with his birthday present.'

He had better be, I thought.

The watch bag was unbelievably heavy and it was then I realised with horror that I had to negotiate Costa, H&M, two tubes, a train and the school run without losing £28,000 worth of watch. And all this before I've even started to write up the report. I couldn't do this every day.

*

When faced with a plethora of shops all appearing to offer the same kind of thing, it helps to be armed with a thick skin and a healthy knowledge of what works best for you and your lifestyle. Many women don't have the time to spend hours traipsing from shop to shop, and many don't enjoy the experience of trying on clothes.

For those whose size isn't within the standard 8–14 range, shopping trips can be an even greater trauma, although collections for fuller sizes have improved in the last twenty years. Most high-street fashion retailers now offer from a size 6 up to a size 18, but this doesn't always mean the clothes will be suitable. JD Williams, the UK's number one retailer for plus-sized people, is widely considered to be the most successful catalogue and online shopping brand in this market. Their aim is to focus on clothes that fit and flatter regardless of size or shape. The UK plus-size womenswear market is worth an estimated £708 million and sales have grown at an annual rate of 67 per cent over five years. There is definitely a spotlight on those niche markets poorly serviced by the high street, and N Brown – the company who owns JD Williams as well as Simply Be, Jacamo, Figleaves and High and Mighty – reported total group revenue of £818 million for 2014. In 2015, the JD Williams 'Championing the Forgotten Fifties' marketing campaign was shortlisted for a *Drapers* award. The staff employed for these shop branches are recruited as 'personal shoppers' offering, one would hope, the skill and fashion know-how to help those less-confident shoppers to leave with outfits which make them look and feel fabulous.

I had often found myself earwigging in fitting rooms as the occupant of the adjacent cubicle attempts to find herself the perfect outfit. I find it very hard to keep schtum.

Customer to assistant in fitting room: 'What do you think of this dress? I'm not sure about it. I think it makes my hips look bigger . . .'

Assistant, who is quite possibly twenty years younger than the customer: 'Oh I really like that dress, it's one of our bestsellers, it's really nice.'

There is rustling and movement outside the cubicle, the assistant is continuing to deal with new stock, this is just chit-chat.

'Yes, but it doesn't work on me, does it? I need it for a wedding next month. I don't want to feel uncomfortable all day.' The worry in this lady's voice is obvious. There is a loaded pause. I'm frozen in front of the mirror, trousers halfway up my legs, waiting for the next response.

'Do you want to try a bigger size?'

Disaster. Nobody *wants* to try a bigger size. In the past I have taken two size options into the fitting room with me and then not looked at the labels so the size doesn't influence me. We can be daft cows, us women, but whatever makes you feel better. This assistant has yet to learn this.

'Shall I fetch you the 14?'

Well, props to her for offering to go and get something,

but *please* stop saying the size out loud so everyone can hear.

'I'm not sure . . . I just think that maybe this style isn't right for me. It's cutting in under the arms and it's making my stomach look bigger, isn't it?'

The lady next door is sounding so pained that I'm imagining her starting to cry. I'm dying to see what it is she has on so I quickly get dressed, gather up my bags and casually emerge from my cubicle.

The lady is standing in her socks in a dress that isn't doing anything for her at all. This lady is what they call an 'apple' – lovely slim limbs, a good bust, but a bit of a tummy. The dress is knee-length and sleeveless, which is fine, but the neckline is too high and there is a strange feature going on in the midsection, drawing attention to her least loved bit. The colour isn't great either. She is very dark and striking and this muted brown is 'meh'; she would look wonderful in a vivid pink or red, or a bright green.

I want desperately to say, 'You could look so much better, you have fabulous shoulders and your legs are great, show them off! Don't hide yourself away in brown or black, wear red, wear blue, buy amazing show-stopping shoes to make you walk tall, and find the perfect shade of lipstick to set off your eyes!'

I smile at the lady who looks utterly miserable and for a minute I think I'm going to say something, but I hesitate and the moment passes. As I walk away I feel sad that this lady can't see her good points that seem so obvious to me. It's frustrating but most of us are the same, spending so much time focusing on covering up the not-so-great bits that we forget to show off the areas that actually, if pushed on the subject, we really rather like. I overhear the apple lady saying, 'I'm going to leave it for now, I need a coffee, I'm not in the right frame of mind,' and she disappears back behind the curtain, deflated, demoralised and defeated.

When I retrained as a personal shopper and stylist, I found it useful to remember the lady with the great legs in that changing room, as well as those times when I didn't feel confident in clothes because I was worried about being too big or too short or too pregnant. I know what to wear to best flatter my shape, colouring and (to a lesser degree because I will happily wear heels to the playground) lifestyle, because I have learnt the hard way, through trial and error. However, now I am formally trained I know the rules for every body shape, and all those useful little tricks that make dressing well so much easier.

I have, as a mystery shopper, been handed the most inappropriate items to try on which have made me grimace at my reflection and feel thankful I'm not a genuine customer in need. I have also been recommended garments I would never have tried in a million years and yet, thanks to the fresh eye of a keen staff member, is totally transformed once off the hanger.

I so enjoy the process of selecting pieces of clothing and putting outfits together, I started to write a style blog, 'After Carrie', somewhere I could be the one making suggestions and pointing out great buys. I'm also not averse to drawing attention to the more ridiculous side of fashion, the trends so unwearable that inevitably – and thankfully – they die a death, although with any luck not before some eager celebrity has dared to give it a go. I say fair play to them for having the nerve; fashion is supposed to be fun, after all.

More than ever we are living in a world where image and external appearance, whether we like it or not, is of the utmost importance. Where once the acting profession seemed cold and unfeeling for casting people based on what they looked like, now, thanks to online dating and apps such as Tinder, we are attempting to build relationships based on a picture and a left or right swipe. Clothes say so much about a person and yet it is not necessarily what we want them to say. Clothes can flatter and disguise and that in turn can build confidence and respect, but if you don't feel comfortable in what you're wearing then it shows, and the effort is counter-productive. I love helping people to go through their over-stuffed wardrobes to sort the wheat from the chaff and create outfits that work for the person and their lifestyle, and in so doing present the best possible version of themselves every day.

I am very lucky, on many levels, that three years ago I started seeing a man who has an even greater appreciation of clothes than I do. As a photographer with an eye for natural beauty and all its quirks, Rupert loves a finely crafted garment hanging in his cupboard, even if that's literally all it does. I think, although I can't possibly prove, that he enjoys clothes shopping as much as he does watching Arsenal play at home. Best of all, Rupert is not afraid to offer an opinion. Although it's not always what I want to hear, it's always a considered and honest one. We both occasionally splurge on things we don't need and then feel guilty about it – but not so guilty we return it.

As a mystery shopper, your job is to be completely objective, to not let your own feelings about a brand, the location of their shop or one of their employees cloud your judgement. This isn't easy for a human being with their own unique likes and dislikes and mystery shoppers are never completely without their prejudices. The best ones, however, try not to let their prejudices influence their reports.

As a genuine shopper, like many people I am becoming more discerning about the clothes I buy, although not so much because I'm concerned about the planet but rather because I'm older and wiser. I think more carefully about the items I spend my money on because once I became a parent I was instantly less frivolous with my cash. Also, because I have a far better understanding about what colours are best for me, the shapes and cuts I should go for and what I should avoid, I spend less. A certain amount of this comes with trial and error but my training confirmed what I already knew, which is that if you get it right, you will ultimately buy fewer things and therefore save money. I still go into Primark, but I'm more likely to fork out for something I know will last and be worn repeatedly.

I still love our high streets, they are more user-friendly than ever before, even if underneath all the glitz and promotion the shops themselves are paddling madly to keep afloat. Many town centres are pedestrianised, with coffee shops that encourage shoppers to kick back and recharge before spending more hours and pounds in the shops. The shops, or at least those that remain, have taken a bashing over the last few years but you wouldn't know it to look at them. Sadly, there are fewer independent retail outlets on our high streets and their units are being taken over by nail bars, blow-dry bars, eyebrow bars and the occasional pop-up shop. The cutesy brands of the eighties and nineties like Knickerbox and Sock Shop have disappeared and been replaced by international brands such as Intimissimi and Tabio.

And are we as shoppers more savvy now that we have the Internet to do our research on? It's undoubtedly easier to save money thanks to the wealth of discount voucher sites and promotional offers but we also need to keep our wits about us as the retail industry uses ever more clever and subliminal methods to persuade us into their stores, to part with our cash, and come back again and again.

Small children now are so much more savvy. When Jake was three I told him he couldn't go on a coin-operated

Peppa Pig ride because I had no change. His response was, 'Have you got your card?'

Children recognise brands from a young age and know what to order in a Starbucks or a Costa. iPhones are second nature to them and they know how to work the Sky box, they also understand about computers, recycling and pollution. At only just four, Jake came home from his first day at school saying he'd had olives and couscous for lunch and did yoga in PE class. Did couscous even exist in the seventies? It wasn't a hundred years ago we read Peter and Jane books, ate spam and watched Mr Benn, and yet it feels like it. We really are children of the last century.

It's no surprise that in our celebrity-obsessed culture, celebrity offspring are every bit as famous and influential as their high-profile parents. As our access to their silver-lined existence becomes easier through Twitter and Instagram, so social-media junkies like Kim Kardashian, whose popularity has soared thanks to the medium, inevitably show off their children. Baby North West is sent a wardrobe full of clothes from Givenchy, Celine and Lanvin among others, Mummy Kim tweets pictures of it and the whole world wants their babies in Givenchy, Celine and Lanvin. Even Prince William and Kate Middleton have a Twitter account. Kate Middleton can clear the rails at Reiss and Whistles in an afternoon by showcasing one of their pieces. Prince George, aged three, is not far behind with the quaint romper suits and tank tops he wears selling out within hours.

Even I have bought high-end brands for my son, albeit heavily reduced from TK Maxx or BrandAlley. As a mystery shopper I have reported on the outrageously niche childrenswear departments in high-end stores, and the demand for very serious outfits for toddlers is extreme. I have struggled not to laugh while following my brief as 'mum buying a £400 outfit for a three-year-old to wear to a wedding', but there it is. There may be an economic downturn, but where there's a Kardashian or a Beckham, there's someone doing their best to upturn it.

The choices we make when we buy our clothes, the fashions we choose to wear versus those we don't and how and where we wear them provides instant visual communication. Whether we choose to have a hand in it to influence that silent first impression, is up to us. You may care desperately what others make of you based on your sartorial choices, you may not, but for as long as we wear clothes, those clothes will speak volumes about us.

After retraining as a stylist I made the difficult decision to give up mystery shopping. It can be interesting and fun but it isn't possible to make a living solely from this type of work. Even if you are signed up to ten different companies, as I have been, the best you can hope for is a part-time job which, if you carry out perhaps twenty assignments, might earn you a couple of hundred pounds extra a month. Plus, it's a strange way to spend time as a forty-something adult and I have dreaded being caught in the act by someone I know. While there is nothing out of the ordinary about bumping into someone out shopping, it can be a little disquieting if you are in the midst of an enquiry about dog food when said acquaintance knows neither you nor your family has a dog.

I do miss it though. Because the fact is, I love shopping, any kind of shopping. I even enjoy a weekly wander around my local Co-op. My friend Clare and I still meet up for a catch up and shop. We don't go for the two-hour supermarket-sweep shopping sessions in H&M that we did before careers, babies and geography got in the way. Clare, though, still tuts when I hold something up against myself that in her opinion has way too many sequins.

'And these . . .' she says, a look of disbelief etched across her face as she holds up one leopard-print ankle boot, remarkably similar to a pair I had recently bought at a Charlotte Olympia sample sale, '*these* should be burnt.'

I open my mouth to defend the boot already flung back on the display, but think better of it. My cut-price designer ones are far more fabulous than those ones anyway.

'Did I tell you about the dress Rupert bought me for Christmas in Paris?' I ask.

'He bought you a dress in Paris? Oh I knew I liked him, what's it like?' Clare checks the price tag of a biker-style jacket. 'I bought this before Christmas and now it's half price. That's so annoying.'

'It's very Oscar de la Renta, a grey tulle skirt with a fitted silvery off-the-shoulder top. It's so gorgeous. I posted a picture of it on Instagram. I don't know where I'm going to wear it, but he said I should have it anyway, because it's a beautiful thing.' I'm showing off now, about my boyfriend, the Paris dress and my ability to use Instagram, the social-media platform that my goddaughter Jess, Clare's thirteen-year-old daughter, lives on.

Right on cue, Jess appears with a jumper in her hands. 'Can I have this, Mum?' she asks, the tone of her voice suggesting she already knows the answer.

'Didn't I buy you a stripy jumper last week, Jess? Isn't that exactly the same?' asks Clare.

'No, it's not, it's completely different.' Jess is incredulous. Clare sighs and looks at me for solidarity, pursing her lips and then saying under her breath, 'It's *exactly* the same.'

I'm torn because I know money doesn't grow on trees and children can't have everything they want all the time and so on and so forth, but – and Clare and I are the worst when it comes to this – we all love a new thing in our wardrobes and more often than not that thing is merely a variation on a theme of several others already in our wardrobes. So often we become fixated on one particular style and then buy it repeatedly; with me it's dressy dresses, with Clare it's little jackets and cardigans. Each new dress or jacket brings with it the promise of change, of improvement on what you already have. I'm a parent too so I can see it from Clare's perspective but I've not changed *that* much since I was a teenager. What I really want to say is, 'Let her have the flippin' top!'

But I don't. I wander off and leave them to it. No doubt I have all this to come.

It makes me think back to when we were really little. Out shopping on a Saturday morning, Mum and Dad, Hannah, Christophe and me. Prompted by one of us saying we wanted something, Dad would announce, 'You can each have one thing.' The three of us would then go into a mad consumer panic as we ran around the shop trying desperately to make a decision. I would usually have a pretty good idea of what I wanted (having led everyone into the shop in the first place) but would make a show of pretending I hadn't quite made up my mind. Hannah would resolutely make a decision on a toy before changing her mind at the last minute to whatever it was I had chosen. Meanwhile Christophe, the youngest but nobody's fool even then, would pick out a toy that couldn't work properly, in his opinion, without an accessory.

'That's two things, Christophe,' Dad would say, trying to hide his delight at the nerve of the child.

'Ohhhh, but this goes with that, there's no point in having that without this . . .' Christophe would wail, a look of despair on his face.

I haven't changed much since then. But from now on I won't be shopping as the character outlined in a brief written by someone in an office.

There will always be another stripy top, slightly better than the last stripy top but now it will have to work for the real me and my life, impractical high heels, small child and all.

ACKNOWLEDGEMENTS

One thing is for sure, if it were not for the brilliance, faith and persistence of my publisher and friend Hannah MacDonald, I would never have got off my arse to write this book. Hannah, I'm so glad you pushed me. If I was worried about thirty-three years of friendship being tested, I needn't have been, it's been a joy – for me at least. Thank you from the bottom of my heart.

Thanks also to Charlotte Cole at September and copy-editor Justine Taylor; you have the patience of saints. I have been spoiled. Thanks also to Sue Amaradivakara.

There are many people who have given of their precious time to help me with this book, otherwise it might have been merely a lot of hot air about my wardrobe: Sean Farrell, Melanie Traub, Richard Cristofoli, Kevin Knox, Holly Browne, Frederik Willems, Nicola Bryan-Jones, Menina Savic, Eric Musgrave, Tara Sendell, Lucy Walsh, Pascale de l'Eprivier, Jodi Zervos, Isabelle Findlay, Dan Davies, Jessica Norman, Ruby Blower, Jessica Burnham, Steve Wells, Kerry Richardson, Jacquie Payne, Sue Schlesinger, Mary Leonard and Kirsty and Ed Hoskins – thank you so much for sharing your knowledge so willingly.

I don't know where I would be without my wonderful friends, both old and new. There are so many of you I have leaned on and received support from and for that I am eternally grateful. Rich and Clare, you lovely people, I've stolen from your lives for this book, please don't think I'm not grateful . . . but I'm not sorry either. You've both done endless listening and advice giving, thank you.

My wonderful family without whom everything would be meaningless: Hannah, Christophe, Lucy, Phoebe, Curtis, Caleb and Sonny, the best family in the world, I'm so lucky to have you all.

Finally, to those who have lived and breathed this book with me every step of the way providing meals, child-care, love and positivity, never once doubting I could do it; Mum you've made this so much easier – you are a tower of strength and a wonderful role model. Rupert, initially you suggested I was making this process look too easy but I think by now you may have changed your mind. Thank you for being there for me and always having a bottle of rosé in the fridge.

And to my beautiful son Jake. I am more proud of you than you can possibly imagine. You have been so patient and taken the many months, weeks and days of 'not long now, Mummy's nearly finished!' in your stride. Your lust for life, so like your grandpa's, inspires me every day.

REFERENCES

Givenchey's interview in *Vanity Fair* mentioned on page 147 was by Amy Fine Collins, 3 February 2014. The figure on page 171 about Bicester Village were quoted in an article by Hilary Rose in *The Times*, 28 October 2015. The figures about mystery shopping on page 257 are from an article by Willie Osterweil in *The New Inquiry*, 4 June 2012.

ABOUT THE AUTHOR

Emily Stott is a freelance fashion journalist and personal stylist. She has been a mystery shopper for fifteen years during which time she has also worked for Thomas Pink. She says the hardest working item in her wardrobe is her heat tech vest – and the moth repellent. Emily lives in Battersea, London, with her son.